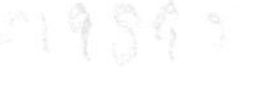

THE BROOKLYN MUSEUM **JAPANESE CERAMICS**

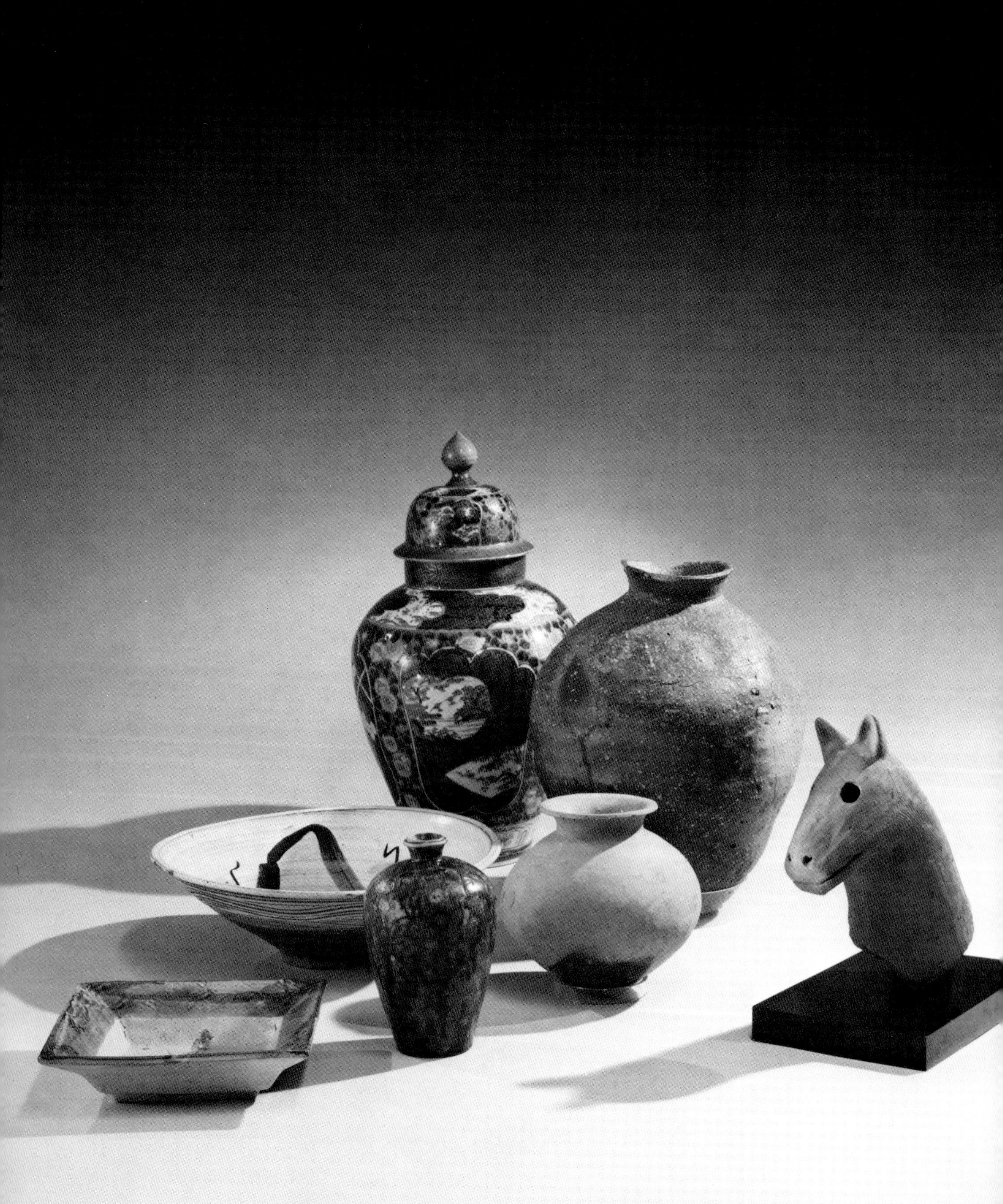

THE BROOKLYN MUSEUM **JAPANESE CERAMICS**

by Robert Moes

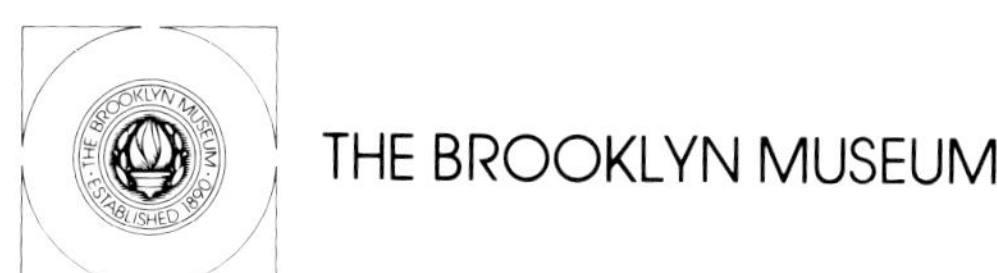

THE BROOKLYN MUSEUM

Published for the exhibition
Japanese Ceramics in The Brooklyn Museum Collection
The Brooklyn Museum, New York
April 25–June 10, 1979

This publication was made possible in part by a grant from the Mary Livingston Griggs and Mary Griggs Burke Foundation and was published as part of the nationwide program Japan Today.

Japan Today *was made possible by grants from the National Endowment for the Humanities, the National Endowment for the Arts, Matsushita Electric (Panasonic), and The Japan Foundation. Sponsored by and organized by: Japan Society, Inc., Meridian House International, and Smithsonian Resident Associate Program.*

Front cover:
Ko-Kutani Ware Dish
Edo Period, second half of the 17th century.
Lent by Dr. John Lyden L79.9.1
[Figure 37]

Back cover:
***Mukōzuke* with Camellia Design**
Edo Period, 18th century.
Ogata Kenzan 1663–1743
Gift of the J. Aron Charitable Foundation 78.208
[Figure 45]

Library of Congress Cataloging in Publication Data
Brooklyn Institute of Arts and Sciences. Museum.
The Brooklyn Museum Japanese ceramics.

Catalog of the exhibition Japanese ceramics in the Brooklyn Museum Collection, Apr. 25–June 10, 1979.
1. Pottery, Japanese—Exhibitions. I. Moes, Robert.
II. Title.
NK4167.B85 1979 738'.0952'074014723 79-10765
ISBN 0-87273-073-5

Designed and published by The Brooklyn Museum, Division of Publications and Marketing Services, Eastern Parkway, Brooklyn, New York 11238. Printed in the USA by the Falcon Press, Philadelphia.

FOREWORD

Michael Botwinick
Director, The Brooklyn Museum

Perhaps the most striking aspect of Japan to the Western world is the Japanese sense of tradition. By now, through exposure in many communications media, we have some idea of the value of tradition in Japanese culture and the extent to which it plays a role in daily life.

Tradition can be seen in two ways. We can speak of the preservation of certain rituals in our lives. The continued use of these rituals can give a sense of direct connection with the past. Tradition may also be seen in the roles that people play—that is to say, in the way they perceive themselves and the way in which they are perceived.

One of the clearest examples of this is in the art of the ceramicist. It is not so much that we see contemporary ceramics as enthralling as objects closely resembling those from earlier times or that we take pleasure in the reappearance of types and their use over generations, but more strongly it is our sense of the timelessness of the artisan. When looking at contemporary Japanese ceramics, one has a sense that the maker stands very much in an unbroken line of many years. His role within society and the extraordinary breadth and subtlety of his aesthetic concerns remain much the same as they were one, two, or three hundred years ago.

On the surface, Japanese ceramics may look quite different from period to period, but in each generation the artist has continued to explore shape and size, form and function, color and shape, decoration and texture. Within the aesthetics of Japanese art, each solution to the questions the artist poses of his craft, in all of its subtleties, is valued most highly as a real addition to the continuing tradition.

This publication was prepared as a part of the NEA-NEH joint program of symposia devoted to contemporary nations. This one, *Japan Today,* involved events and programs in six American cities. The program was coordinated by Japan Society, Inc., in New York. We are grateful for the opportunity of having been involved in this celebration and hope we have made some small contribution.

UNDERSTANDING JAPANESE CERAMICS

Robert Moes

Japan is the only country in the world where ceramics are considered fine art, every bit as important as painting and sculpture. What are the further characteristics which distinguish Japanese art from that of other countries? What is unique about Japanese art? What is *Japanese* about Japanese art?

Because of its diversity, Japanese art defies totally valid generalizations; nearly every rule will be found to have exceptions. Nevertheless, there are certain basic attitudes that set Japanese art apart.

One such attitude is *directness,* a tendency to go right to the thing itself rather than to intellectualize. Directness is a key to the Japanese genius for design. The artist takes motifs directly from nature and gives them comprehensible, simplified forms that enhance their natural beauty (see Fig. 8). He juxtaposes these forms in bold, imaginative, harmonious ways. He works directly and sympathetically with his materials, taking advantage of their natural properties rather than refining them beyond recognition (see Fig. 12). The viewer, in turn, enjoys the work of art directly, deriving deep satisfaction from its formal aspects.

Such directness is notably different from prevailing attitudes in the arts of both India and China, from whom Japan borrowed many cultural elements. From India came Buddhism, with its complex iconography and anthropomorphic representations of deities. But the Indian preoccupation with spiritual values and the belief that reality is illusory has produced a cultural pattern in India of passive inaction quite different from the assertiveness and industriousness of the Japanese. Buddhism fulfills an emotional need in Japan, but denying reality runs counter to most Japanese feelings. Rather than deny what they see around them, the Japanese tend to accept it with gratitude and enjoy its beneficial aspects. Shintō, the indigenous religion of Japan, is in part an expression of appreciation and respect for the hospitable natural environment of the Japanese islands. According to Shintō mythology, the islands were created by the gods, and their inhabitants descended from the Sun Goddess. There is a *kami* (spirit) within every rock, tree, mountain, or blade of grass.

During several periods in its history, Japan has borrowed many of the external manifestations of Chinese culture, but its basic values have remained very different from those of China. Although Chinese pragmatism is quite unlike Indian denial of the illusory world, the Chinese do have a predilection for moral philosophy and intellectualization that is at variance with the more direct, intuitive, and emotional approach of the Japanese.

Linearity, flatness, and patternization are general characteristics of Japanese art (see Fig. 64). Painting with line and areas of flat color instead of creating an illusion of volume by modeling in light and shade distinguishes Japanese painting from that of the West. Transitory effects such as cast shadows normally are not represented.

India produces a great deal of sculpture. The bodies of Indian deities are not human bodies, but assemblages of idealized natural forms used as metaphors for divine perfection. The swelling volumes of Indian sculpture are conceived as if expanded by inner spiritual power. Japanese sculpture, by comparison, is more linear, more involved with contours and patterns than with volume.

Just as the body of an Indian deity is a metaphor for divine perfection, so is a Chinese landscape painting a metaphor for all of nature and its inherent order, as well as an expression of the noble sentiments of scholar-artists.

Japan welcomed Chinese landscape painting just as it welcomed Buddhist sculpture: at face value, so to speak. The welcome was enthusiastic and sincere, but without a deep understanding of the subtle symbolism of the paintings. Shintō appreciation of nature was sufficient reason to paint landscapes. Buddhist images answer a spiritual need, since Shintō deities are normally not represented in anthropomorphic form. The mountain, tree, or rock in which the *kami* dwells is his embodiment, or a bronze mirror may be used as his symbol. Japan's rich sculptural tradition is entirely due to the introduction of Buddhism.

Although their basic modes of drawing are the same, Japanese painters do not share the Chinese interest in spatial recession and enveloping atmosphere. The Japanese are more interested in surface pattern and decorative effect. Under the influence of Confucian moral philosophy, Chinese artists used to paint figures who were models of virtuous conduct, such as great administrators and scholars. The Japanese preferred more romantic narratives showing the deeds of great warriors, priests, or lovers. Ordinary people were painted with accurate observation and empathy, not as models of ideal behavior or manifestations of the gods, but delighted in for their own sake, *directly.*

Another significant factor that distinguishes Japanese art from Chinese art is Japan's respect for the crafts. In old China, only painting and calligraphy were considered art. This was essentially an elitist concept, since painting and calligraphy were the arts practiced by the intellectual aristocracy, those Confucian-trained scholar-officials whose main job was government administration. Because China's art critics and arbiters of taste were these same scholar-officials, even the work of professional painters was excluded from the realm of art. Professional painters were considered mere artisans, no better than the craftsmen who painted designs on porcelain, or worked jade, or cast bronzes. This condescending view of craftsmen derived from literati painting theory, according to which only a scholar-gentleman had the education, nobility of spirit, and freedom from commercial need to produce a true work of art.

The prevailing attitude in Japan is entirely different. The work of a great potter (see Fig. 56) is considered just as significant as the work of a great painter. An artist is a craftsman and a good craftsman is an artist. A painter or calligrapher is not placed in a special category; he is merely a craftsman pursuing a different trade from, say, a potter.

The distinction made in the West between the "fine arts" (painting, sculpture, architecture) and the "crafts" (ceramics, metalwork, furniture, glass, lacquer, basketry, weaving, dyeing) has no meaning in Japan. Only in 1871, after the reopening of Japan to the outside world and the beginning of Westernization, did the Japanese finally coin a word for "fine art." The concept simply did not exist before the introduction of Western ideas. To the Japanese, a painter or sculptor or architect was a craftsman, just as a potter or swordsmith was. A sword blade was both an embodiment of military valor and a beautiful work of art. A somber, uneven, glazed pottery tea bowl made by a humble immigrant Korean potter (see Fig. 18) embodied the highest ideals of art.

This Japanese respect for the craftsman and his work is related to Japan's appreciation of nature. The craftsman's product is a modified natural substance; iron-bearing river sand and charcoal fire becomes a sword; mud and pine-bough fire becomes a tea bowl. The *kami* of the forge or kiln participates in the craftsman's work, and offerings of rice and wine are placed on a small shrine shelf attached to the kiln.

One of the most attractive characteristics of Japanese art is its direct and sympathetic use of natural materials (see Fig. 6). The sensitivity with which a Japanese craftsman responds to wood, clay, paper, lacquer, bamboo, iron, bronze, or cloth is breathtaking. This, together with the magnificent Japanese sense of design, has produced some of the most aesthetically satisfying works of art in the world. The Japanese craftsman's customer takes delight in the craftsman's skillful use of natural materials, and the craftsman derives deep satisfaction from his work. Japan's love of nature and respect for the *kami* in natural materials are important in its unique appreciation of crafts.

The Japanese respect for the craftsman also derives from an empathy with ordinary people and an old, conservative social system that sought to maintain an absolute status quo. In this system, the relationship between a craftsman and his apprentices has always been nearly as important as that between a *samurai* and his retainers. The apprentices gain a deep knowledge of their craft and a legendary skill with their hands through a long period of traditional training. Only when technique has become second nature is it possible to create truly direct and inspired works of art. Such professionalism is widely at variance with the Chinese ideal of the artist as scholarly amateur.

Western-style industrialization in the late nineteenth century threatened to destroy Japan's great crafts traditions, but the Folk Art Movement, begun by Yanagi Sōetsu about 1918, has succeeded in restoring Japanese respect for crafts and insuring the continuation of crafts traditions. Japan is now the world's leader in ceramics. Legions of potters from Europe and America go to Japan for study or imitate Japanese techniques at home.

Another characteristic of Japanese art is the acceptance of, even the preference for, effects of wear and age on objects. For example, the wooden columns and beams in Buddhist temples are hardly ever repainted. Most of the red paint has long ago worn off, exposing the bare wood, which weathers to a handsome natural patina. There is just a trace of the old paint, much darkened with age, in protected nooks and crannies, which complements the weathered wood. The Japanese much prefer this mellow, varigated effect to the harsher appearance of the original paint. The wooden columns and beams of Shintō shrines and Japanese houses are left as exposed wood except under rare instances of Buddhist influence. Their surfaces are never touched up with rasps or sandpaper but are trimmed with razor-sharp draw-knives to a velvety smoothness and then allowed to slowly weather.

An effect similar to that of worn-off paint was achieved intentionally on a type of Japanese lacquer ware called Negoro (after the Negoro-dera monastery where it was supposedly first used). The wood surface of an object was first coated with black lacquer and then with red lacquer. The red layer was subsequently polished away in random areas, exposing the black underneath for a rich, mellow effect that looked like the result of great age and frequent use. Of course, this effect must originally have occurred accidentally, for red-lacquered wares often had an undercoat of black lacquer. But the Japanese admired the naturally worn effect and began producing it on new pieces.

Japanese admiration for the effects of wear and age on objects is related to Japan's sensitive use of natural materials. Both come from the appreciation of nature. They also reflect Japanese pragmatism, an inclination to accept things the way they are and enjoy them for what they are. This is quite different from India's concept of an illusory world and Indians' consequent retreat into the spiritual realm.

Admiration for the effects of wear and age also relates to a Japanese preference for asymmetry and irregularity in design, a preference that contrasts sharply with the Chinese love for symmetry and order. Chinese designs tend to repeat formally on either side of a central axis, while Japanese designs tend to be more informal, irregular, and asymmetrical.

Japanese interest in age, wear, asymmetry, and irregularity finds its most complete expression in the tea bowl (Fig. 18), the most uniquely Japanese of all objects. One of Chōjirō's Black Raku tea bowls is like a man-made object returning to nature, an intentionally distorted, glazed-pottery drinking bowl that resembles an ancient, smoothly worn river stone. The whole tea ceremony cult developed around this Japanese aesthetic. The words *sabi* ("patina, age, antique appearance") and *wabi* ("aesthetic appreciation of the irregular and understated") were adapted to describe these effects.

Zen Buddhism, with its spontaneous, intuitive awareness of reality, is usually mentioned as the source of the tea-ceremony aesthetic. There is some truth in this. Several of the great tea masters were Zen monks. In Japan, both the tea ceremony and Zen Buddhism developed under the patronage of the military aristocracy. However, Ch'an (Zen) Buddhism in China, whence Japan's came, never produced an intentionally distorted tea bowl. That required the direct and appreciative Japanese response to nature plus exposure to Korean peasant rice bowls of the sixteenth century.

Another primary characteristic of Japanese art is its variety. Nothing could be further from Chōjirō's Black Raku tea bowl than Kaihō Yūshō's peony screen, with its bold use of gold leaf and bright colors. Yet both were produced about the same time under the same kind of patronage. One finds similar aesthetic opposites throughout much of the history of Japanese art: luxurious ostentation (see Fig. 32) versus refined understatement (see Fig. 18), delicate and elaborate ornamentation (see Fig. 35) versus broad, simple effects (see Fig. 46).

The Japanese language is rich in words for a wide variety of aesthetic categories. Such words frequently defy exact translation. We have noted that *sabi* and *wabi* refer to aspects of tea-ceremony taste. At the opposite aesthetic pole is *hade,* meaning "gorgeous, bright, ostentatious." *Shibui* ("quiet, restrained, harmonious") is less extreme than *sabi* or *wabi* and not as closely related to the tea ceremony; it literally means "astringent," like the taste of a slightly unripe persimmon. The muted gray or somber tan *kimono* with quiet, simple patterns worn by older women are *shibui.* They have a calm beauty that is more satisfying than that of the gorgeous, elaborate *kimono* worn by younger women. *Jimi* ("subdued, unpretentious") is a little less astringent than *shibui,* meaning something more like "quiet good taste." *Iki* means "chic."

Victorian Westerners responded enthusiastically to the more elaborate Japanese art but heartily condemned the understated. In the mid-twentieth century, some Westerners have over-emphasized the subdued aspects of Japanese art, seeing in them the true expression of the Japanese sensibility. Actually, both poles of Japanese taste are equally characteristic. One may draw a parallel between these two aesthetic poles and two seemingly contradictory aspects of the Japanese personality: sensitivity to subtle aesthetic nuances and determination and aggressiveness.

Japan abounds in contradictions. We have spoken of directness in Japanese art, yet indirectness is prevalent in Japan. In government and business, real power is often wielded behind the scenes. Japanese etiquette usually deals with delicate matters in indirect ways. There is a general tendency to formalize things, to turn relatively simple procedures, such as the tea ceremony or merely buying a train ticket, into virtual rituals. In the Nō drama, actions and emotions are expressed indirectly through stately mime and dance. Even in the more popular and boisterous Kabuki, the acting is highly stylized. Hereditary schools of acting, the tea ceremony, and painting have evolved complex formal rules. Creativity and artistic growth may have been stifled in a few cases, but viable traditions have been maintained and brilliant individual artists have emerged continually.

Indirectness also abounds in Japanese poetry and prose, where allusions, metaphors, and symbols are everywhere. Certain birds, insects, plants, garments, colors, and smells have come to suggest certain emotions, moods, or even situations. The most extreme nuances of this highly refined language of symbols formerly occurred in the literature of the court nobility, but even then, most Japanese knew much of it and responded automatically. This vocabulary of symbols has been transmitted to painting and the decorative arts, enriching them with multiple levels of meaning.

Buddhist concepts about the transitory nature of life and the prevailing sadness of things (*mono-no-aware*) have added poignancy and urgency to the symbols, thereby heightening the perception of beauty. Wild geese, for example, suggest the autumn season, the time when they pass through Japan on their way south for the winter. Autumn in turn calls to mind the evanescence of life in this world. Cherry blossoms connote spring, but they too suggest transitoriness, because the petals fall away a few days after the blossoms open. Fallen cherry petals symbolize fallen warriors, *samurai* who died in battle serving their feudal lords. Japanese admire the beauty of a fallen leaf as much as that of the ones still on the tree. One of their favorite colors is *kareha-iro* ("dead-leaf brown").

Another characteristic contradiction in Japanese culture is a tendency to enthusiastically welcome new trends, whether imported or Japanese, while rigorously preserving and perpetuating older traditions. Japan welcomed Buddhism but never discarded Shintō, and today most Japanese nominally belong to both faiths. Marriages are performed by Shintō priests, but funerals are conducted by Buddhist monks. Even within Japanese Buddhism, one finds an astonishing array of radically different schools that were imported independently from the continent. Three in particular fulfill strong Japanese spiritual needs: Shingon, with its mystery and ritual, Jōdo and Shin, with their easy salvation for the masses, and Zen, with its more difficult and personal intuitive enlightenment.

The Japanese energetically sought several successive waves of massive cultural influence from China, yet never sacrificed their native individuality or rejected their past. Imported Chinese objects were imitated directly at first, with remarkable but characteristic dexterity, then gradually assimilated into the national heritage and altered to suit Japanese usage. Today all the latest styles of contemporary American painting are imitated immediately by some Japanese artists, while others go right on working in time-honored native traditions. Swordsmiths still forge magnificent swords in Japan in an age when swords no longer have a practical purpose.

Another general characteristic of Japanese art is localism. Each region, each city, and ultimately each village used to have its own special way of doing things (see Fig. 14). Until modern times, communication within Japan was not easy. Although the many rivers and bays and the Inland Sea and the oceans do provide a network of waterways for commerce and communication, they also break Japan up into a profusion of separate islands and districts. Broad plains and rolling hills appear in certain places, but much of the islands' surfaces are occupied by rugged mountains that further divide the country into small areas. Under Japan's feudal system, from the late twelfth century through the mid-nineteenth, there were political barriers as well; the nation was divided into numerous fiefs, which were often at war with one another. Even during peaceful times, travel from one fief to another was usually restricted. However, the resulting situation was not detrimental to the arts and crafts, for it produced a startling variety of vigorous local traditions. Even today each district and nearly every town has its *meibutsu*, or famous local product, which the Japanese traveler brings home as the obligatory *omiyage* ("souvenir gift"). A current fad in Japan, where people have always loved to travel within their own country, is "Discover Japan" tours for the Japanese. Unhappily, however, modern industrial technology is gradually destroying local traditions and substituting insipid standardization.

Japan has been unusually fortunate in being able to pursue its own course of development without much interference. Japan's geographic isolation from the mainland saved it from the hordes of invaders who swept across China and Korea. Yet Japan's isolation was not complete; it could exchange goods and ideas with the continent as it chose, closing its doors to the outside world during certain periods and communicating with it actively during others. The first Europeans visited Japan in 1542 and were followed by hundreds of missionaries and traders. But the Japanese government saw the potential threat of conquest and colonization, and gradually expelled all Westerners except the Dutch (see Fig. 33), who were allowed to maintain a small trading station at Nagasaki. Not until Commodore Perry forced the reopening of Japanese ports in the mid-nineteenth century did Japan suffer the indignity of serious foreign interference in internal affairs. After Perry's visit, the Japanese, with characteristic determination, turned their ancient feudal society into a modern industrial nation almost overnight.

Awareness and appreciation of art is considerably more widespread in Japan than in many other countries. One never fails to see laborers and housewives as well as businessmen, professional people, students, and collectors at Japanese art galleries and museums. Enthusiasm for art runs high. For years it has been common in Japan to find three-block-long lines of people waiting for entry to art exhibitions, a phenomenon only recently seen in the United States. Supplying the public demand for art is big business in Japan. In addition to the public art museums in nearly every city, there are countless small private art museums open to the public for a nominal admission fee several months a year. Japanese department stores compete with one another in staging art exhibitions of all types, held in special galleries right in the stores themselves. Japanese corporations constantly sponsor major art exhibitions and publish lavish catalogues.

A partial explanation for Japan's deep awareness of art is the splendid old tradition of school art excursions (*shūgaku ryokō*). Nearly every Japanese child goes frequently with his classes to visit important temples, shrines, gardens, and art museums. But it is more than participation in school tours that has made Japan a whole nation of art lovers. The Japanese simply have a natural inclination to enjoy art. Their love of nature sustains their awareness of beauty and their Buddhist idea of transitoriness heightens it. In Japan, *biteki kōsatsu* ("aesthetic contemplation, looking at art") is both a high ideal and a favorite pastime.

The Jōmon Period circa 10,000 – 300 B.C.

It is intriguing to note that Japan, the only country where ceramics are considered fine art, the only country where a good potter can make a decent living without resorting to teaching or other outside work, is also the country where the oldest known pottery remains have been found. Radiocarbon dating of associated organic material and thermoluminescence testing of the clay itself have yielded dates of approximately 10,000 B.C. for the earliest Jōmon pottery. Presumably, this pottery had mainland antecedents, the remains of which have not yet been discovered.

It is also significant that pottery vessels are the most interesting and characteristic remains from the Jōmon Period, and that the name for this phase of Japanese cultural history refers to a technique used to decorate pottery: "Jōmon" means "cord-pattern" (see Fig. 1).

Edward S. Morse, an American zoologist brought from Boston to teach at the Tokyo Imperial University after Japan reopened her ports to the outside world, is called the Father of Japanese Archaeology. In 1879 he excavated the shell mounds at Ōmori, near the railway line between Tokyo and Yokohama. He found around Tokyo several partially buried large shell heaps and surmised that these marked the sites of Stone Age villages.

Pre-Neolithic (pre-pottery) remains in Japan are sparse, but some elephant fossils have been found that seem to indicate Japan was once connected by a land bridge across the Straits of Tsushima to the tip of the Korean peninsula and the Asiatic mainland beyond. Japan may also have once been connected through the Ryukyus to the Philippines and Java, and Paleolithic and Mesolithic men probably were able to walk across to Japan.

Stone tools about 500,000 years old have been discovered in Kyūshū, the large southern island of the Japanese archipelago. Others, about 200,000 years old, have been found in Gumma Prefecture, not far north of Tokyo. One reason so few such remains have turned up is that these early settlers lived near the coasts , and the continual rising and falling of the land has submerged or buried most of them

The Jōmon people, on the other hand, left extensive remains. Over two thousand shell mounds (the garbage heaps beside their villages) have been excavated. They have been found all over the Japanese islands but are most abundant in the Kantō Plain, the area around Tokyo where about half the known sites are located. By carefully sifting through the debris in these kitchen middens and excavating the village sites next to them, archaeologists have learned a good deal about Jōmon culture, which seems to have lasted from about 10,000 B.C. to about 300 B.C. in the southwestern part of Japan but to have persisted until as late as about A.D. 1000 in the northeast, where Jōmon people who resisted subjugation or absorption by later settlers were pushed by succeeding migrations of more culturally advanced people from the mainland. Well into the Fujiwara Period (A.D. 894–1185), the Japanese were still fighting border skirmishes with Jōmon descendants in the far northeastern provinces.

It was once thought that the Ainu, Caucasian aborigines on Hokkaidō, the large northern Japanese island, were descended from the Jōmon people. This theory is now regarded with suspicion because Ainu culture has only been traced back about three hundred years, leaving a gap of over six hundred years between the latest Jōmon remains and the earliest known Ainu ones. Nevertheless, there may be a very general connection: as Japanese civilization spread northeast to the upper coast of Honshū, the large central island, a few Jōmon descendants may have moved across to Hokkaidō.

Jōmon culture is classified as Proto-Neolithic rather than Neolithic because the Jōmon people made pottery and polished stone tools but had no agriculture. They lived by gathering game, fish, fruit, nuts, berries, and roots. A few of their villages were in the mountains, but the majority were near the sea coasts or by the banks of rivers; they relied heavily on marine or river shellfish for food. Agriculture became known only in the very late stages of Jōmon culture through contact with the more advanced peoples who began taking over southwestern Japan around 300 B.C.

The Jōmon people probably began arriving in Japan about 10,000 B.C., having presumably come from the mainland in dugout canoes. The standard Jōmon architectural type, the pit house, is similar to examples found in Siberia, so the Jōmon people may have come from northeast Asia, either by way of Korea or directly from the Siberian coast to the northern Japanese islands. The fact that their remains are more prevalent around Tokyo than in Kyūshū, near Korea, may indicate that they arrived in the north and moved southwest until later arrivals drove them northeast again.

Jōmon pottery vessels have been unearthed all over Japan. There are regional variations, but these are less important than chronological stylistic development, which Japanese scholars have divided into five phases: Earliest Jōmon (*circa* 4500–3700 B.C.), Early Jōmon (*circa* 3700–3000 B.C.), Middle Jōmon (*circa* 3000–2000 B.C.; see Fig 1), Late Jōmon (*circa* 2000–1000 B.C.; see Fig. 2), and Latest Jōmon (*circa* 1000–250 B.C.; see Fig. 3). All the types have certain characteristics in common. They were made by coiling; the potter's wheel was not yet known. They were fired in open pits; there were not yet kilns. Jōmon pottery is extremely porous, low-fired earthenware, unsuitable for holding liquids for any length of time. The clay was rather poorly refined and glazes were unknown. A few of the Latest Jōmon vessels were covered with a lacquer-like substance.

The principal means of decorating Jōmon pottery was to press various kinds of twisted cord against the clay surface before firing so as to create rows of indentations. Parallel diagonal rows of cord impressions were the most common (see Fig. 1). As the technique developed, cord was wrapped around cylindrical or paddle-shaped spatulas used to beat patterns into the clay. Pressed-cord decoration is found on vessels from all five stages of the Jōmon chronology.

Cord-marking was not the only technique used to decorate Jōmon pottery. Textured stick ends or irregular seashell edges were also used to make impressions on clay surfaces, and spatulas with carved surfaces were used to beat designs into the clay. Borders between zones of cord-pattern were created by carving or scraping the clay; these techniques were also used independently of cord-marking. Rouletting (rolling a carved or cord-wrapped wood cylinder over the soft clay) was also employed. Some of the most vigorous Jōmon decoration was done with applied clay strands, which eventually developed into bold, flamboyant sculptural forms extending well above vessel rims (see Fig. 1).

Pottery vessels from the Earliest Jōmon Period consist of simple conical beakers or pointed-bottomed bowls unable to stand by themselves. They are decorated with patterns of incised or cord-impressed lines.

In the Early Jōmon Period, potters coiled vessel walls up from the perimeters of clay disks instead of starting from points, producing flat bottoms that allowed pots to stand by themselves. A tall, cylindrical-beaker shape was most common. Decoration became somewhat more sophisticated, with the textured surface pattern divided into bands or horizontal zones by incised lines or rows of stamped dots. Vessel rims were sometimes articulated with broad cusps. Applied clay dabs and small strips began to appear.

In the Middle Jōmon Period, the decoration of pottery vessels became quite exuberant (see Fig. 1). So flamboyant did the applied clay ornamentation sometimes become that it rendered vessels useless for ordinary utilitarian purposes. Such elaborate vessels must have been made for ritual use. The designs on more utilitarian pots probably also had magical significance.

Pottery from the Late and Latest Jōmon Periods (Figs. 2 and 3) is somewhat tame compared to the vigor of Middle Jōmon. The bold applied-clay forms leaping above vessel rims and articulating their sides went out of vogue.

Curvilinear zones of cord-impressed texture alternating with smooth clay surfaces became standard. Vessel shapes became more varied than in earlier times.

Jōmon figurines (*dogū;* Figs. 4 and 5), usually only a few inches tall, are made of the same clay as the vessels. Their highly stylized forms bear little relation to actual anatomy, but nearly all of the figurines are clearly female and tend to have accentuated body parts having to do with childbearing, such as breasts and pubic areas. Jōmon figurines are thus almost certainly female fertility fetishes analogous to the stone or clay Mother Goddess images made in Europe, the Near East, and India during the Stone Age and later. The well-known European "Venus" figures of about 15,000 B.C. have exaggerated thighs and abstract faces similar to those of many Jōmon figurines.

Few figurines are known from Earliest Jōmon. A rare stone figurine has survived from the Early Jōmon period, and a small number of clay figurines from Middle Jōmon have come down to us. The most famous has seemingly feline features in the pronounced stylization of its face. Several examples of similar faces have survived, not from figurines but from "rim heads," hollow protrusions on the rims of clay vessels. Late Jōmon figurines are abundant (Fig. 4). The most typical type has a flat, cookie cutter appearance. One unique and spectacular example has a concave, heart-shaped face expressive of intense magic power. The incised or impressed parallel lines, circles, and rows of dots on the surfaces of Jōmon figurines no doubt represent actual body painting and tattooing. Chronicles of the Han Dynasty (206 B.C.–A.D. 221) in China mention such practices by the Japanese, and they are still in vogue among the Ainu.

Clay figurines from the Latest Jōmon period are the most common type (Fig. 5). They have bulbous thighs reminiscent of the Stone Age European Venus figures, as well as linear or relief emphasis on the breasts and pubic areas. Their surfaces are covered with curvilinear patterns made up of areas of pressed-cord markings with scraped or incised borders. A striking feature of Latest Jōmon figurines are their huge, bulging, horizontally slit eyes, suggestive of potent spiritual energy. The nose is often absent altogether, and the mouth is reduced to a dot. The eyes become the whole face. This peculiar stylization of the eyes once gave rise to a theory that they represented wooden snow goggles like those used by the Eskimos. However, snowfall is rather light in the parts of Japan where most of the Jōmon remains have been found. A somewhat more plausible theory maintains that these eyes derive from earlier figurines that had eyes made of cowry shells like those of sculpture from the South Pacific Islands.

The Yayoi Period circa 300 B.C. — circa A.D. 300

In 1884 a pottery jar of unfamiliar type was dug up in Yayoi-machi, Hongo-ku (now Bunkyo-ku), Tokyo. The name "Yayoi" was officially adopted for Japan's Bronze-Iron Age in 1902, by which time much more had been learned about this period.

The Yayoi people seem to have migrated across the Straits of Tsushima from the southern tip of Korea to the northwest corner of Kyūshū by boat. Yayoi culture was technologically superior to Jōmon. The Yayoi people manufactured metal tools and weapons, practiced agriculture, and domesticated animals. They spread throughout Kyūshū and the southern half of Honshū, subjugating, absorbing, and driving out the Jōmon people.

Yayoi agriculture consisted primarily of wet-paddy rice farming, the same method used in China, Korea, and Japan today. The technique probably developed in South China, then spread northward as far as Korea, whence it was brought to Japan. A few grains of rice have left impressions on artifacts excavated from Yayoi sites; the type of rice is related to one grown in east central China between the Yellow River and the Yangtze. The Yayoi people also raised horses, cattle, and chickens.

Japan really had no separate Bronze Age. Early Yayoi people arriving from Korea introduced fully developed bronze technology, and iron followed within a few years. Throughout the remainder of the Yayoi Period, ordinary metal tools and weapons were made of iron, while ceremonial and ritual ones were bronze. The many Yayoi bronze weapons that have been excavated must be votive objects; their blades are too large and thin for combat use.

The Yayoi people seem to have been of Mongoloid racial stock; the Jōmon people seem to have been Caucasoid. The modern Japanese are racially heterogeneous, composed mainly of Mongoloid stock with an admixture of Caucasoid and Negrito (South Sea Island) elements. This accounts for the wide variety of facial types one sees among the Japanese.

Yayoi bronze and iron utensils were eventually made locally in Japan, but quantities were also imported from Korea. The latter included many bronze objects exported to Korea from Han Dynasty China.

A Yayoi ruler in Japan sent an emissary to the Han Court. According to the Chinese chronicle *Book of Later Han,* an envoy from the state of Nu in Wa (Japan) arrived in A.D. 57 and was given a seal by Emperor Kuang Wu. A gold seal discovered in North Kyūshū in 1789 bears the inscription: "King of Nu of Wa, [Vassal of] Han."

A later Chinese chronicle mentions the Japanese at about the end of the Yayoi Period. *Account of the Three Kingdoms,* recorded shortly before A.D. 297, says that the people of Wa were law-abiding, fond of liquor, agricultural, good at spinning and weaving, skilled at fishing, and maintained strict social distinctions. The account tells us there were one hundred Wa countries (tribes) of one thousand to seventy thousand households each, some with kings, others with queens, and that thirty Wa countries were in communication with China.

Yayoi pottery (Fig. 6) is more functional and utilitarian than Jōmon. Because the Jōmon people lacked metal, their ceremonial objects included large, elaborate clay vessels. In Yayoi times objects indicative of status or intended for ritual use were made of bronze.

Yayoi ceramics were technically more advanced than Jōmon. They were still earthenware, but they were fired in kilns and made of a better refined clay, thus avoiding the extreme porosity of Jōmon vessels. The Yayoi conquerors no doubt employed Jōmon potters, for early Yayoi pottery is similar to Latest Jōmon Period ware in Kyūshū.

By middle Yayoi times, a rudimentary potter's wheel came into use, but larger vessels continued to be built by coiling. The walls of pots became thinner and more uniform. Shapes began to resemble those of Korea, whence the potter's wheel had come to Japan. A wide variety of utilitarian forms were produced. Decoration consisted mainly of incised grooves, combed patterns, impressed cord or shell edges, and painted slip (liquid clay), used either on the design itself or on the background.

The Tomb Period circa A.D. 300 — 552

The most characteristic remains from the Tomb Period are gigantic mound tombs and their contents; hence the name of the period, called Kofun ("old tumulus") in Japanese. In English, the term Proto-historic Period is also used because of the introduction of Chinese writing by Korean scribes at the Japanese Court during the Tomb Period. History, formerly transmitted by professional reciters as oral tradition, gradually was committed to writing during this era.

Chinese writing is said to have been introduced in Japan in A.D. 405. At first, written Chinese was used in its original form. In the eighth century, however, certain Chinese characters were employed for their sound value, regardless of their meaning, and combined to approximate the sounds of Japanese words, thus permitting Japanese poetry to be written down for the first time. In the ninth century some of the radicals (elements) of Chinese characters were adapted as syllabaries to represent the fifty basic sounds of spoken Japanese. In modern written Japanese, main words are written with Chinese ideographs; helping words, verb and adjectival endings, and foreign words are written with syllabaries.

Although written records were kept from about A.D. 405 onwards, none of the earliest histories have survived. The oldest extant Japanese chronicles were committed to writing in the early eighth century: the Kojiki (Record of Ancient Matters) in 712, and the Nihon Shoki (History of Japan, also called the Nihongi) in 720. These two chronicles trace Japanese history back to the age of the gods and have much to say about events during the Tomb Period. They incorporate earlier writings as well as orally transmitted material. In the Kojiki and Nihon Shoki, myth and history mingle freely.

The Kojiki and Nihon Shoki scarcely mention the Jōmon and Yayoi peoples, for these are the chronicles of the Yamato clans, and other groups are mentioned mainly as barbarian tribes requiring subjugation. The chronicles tell us that Ninigi-no-Mikoto, grandson of Amaterasu (the Sun Goddess), descended from the plains of heaven to Kyūshū, carrying the Imperial regalia (the mirror, sword, and jewel) with him. In 660 B.C. Jimmu Tennō, Ninigi's great-grandson, became the first emperor. He led his warriors north from Kyūshū, conquered local tribes along the Inland Sea, and settled in the Yamato plain (the Kyoto-Nara-Osaka region). It was a common early practice to push things further back in time to gain the added prestige of greater antiquity, and the events detailed in the chronicles must have taken place around A.D. 300 rather than 660 B.C..

The Yamato clans did not, of course, actually descend to Japan from heaven as the chronicles would have it. They were, in fact, pastoral, equestrian warrior tribes from Korea who migrated across the Straits of Tsushima to Japan in the fourth century and managed to subjugate the earlier settlers. One of the Yamato clan chiefs became the first Japanese emperor, probably after fighting his way up the Inland Sea from Kyūshū as is related in the chronicles.

Japanese culture changed radically in the fourth century A.D. Earlier burials had been in simple graves, small stone-lined chambers, or mouth-to-mouth pottery jars. Suddenly, beginning in the early fourth century, large mounds of earth were constructed above all major tombs, a practice that was already standard in southeast Korea. All sorts of luxury goods were placed in the tomb chamber to serve the deceased chieftain in the spirit world. These objects were virtually identical to Korean examples of the Silla Period (57 B.C.–A.D. 668). It is obvious that the Silla and Yamato warriors had common ancestors who migrated to southeast Korea from Manchuria, Mongolia, and the steppes of Central Asia.

The Tomb Period has two distinct ceramic traditions, one imported from Korea, the other indigenous. The first, Sue Ware (*sueki;* Fig. 7), appeared in the late fourth or early fifth century. It is nearly identical to Silla stoneware of the fourth to sixth centuries. The similarity is so close that pieces of unknown provenance are sometimes difficult to classify as to whether they are Japanese or Korean. Sue Ware was no doubt actually used by the aristocrats of the Tomb Period, but it was also a funerary ware (specifically made to be deposited in tombs). Virtually all of the surviving Sue pots have been recovered from tombs (there were as many as 210 in one burial), no doubt because those for everyday use were broken and discarded.

Sue Ware is considerably more technically advanced than Jōmon and Yayoi pottery. It is not earthenware but is a hard, high-fired, nonporous gray stoneware, thrown on a rapidly rotating potter's wheel. The relatively high firing temperature frequently induced patches of accidental ash glaze. Wood ash falling on the ware during firing acted as a flux, causing silica in the clay to fuse into a rudimentary greenish glaze on parts of the surface. Potters soon learned to control and use ash glaze intentionally.

The most typical Sue pot is a bowl or jar supported by a perforated pedestal. Decoration is generally confined to simple combed patterns, ash glaze, or a combination of the two. Some of the funerary pedestal-jars have tiny, pinched-clay figurines of people or animals attached to the shoulders of the jars. This was a Japanese innovation; in Korea the pinched-clay tomb figurines were independent, never attached to vessels. Separate figurines were not deposited in Japanese tombs, but the size and shape of the attached Japanese figurines closely resemble those of the separate ones in Korea.

Sue remained the principal Japanese ceramic ware well into the Fujiwara Period (A.D. 897–1185), but post-sixth century examples (see Fig. 9) are rare because mound tombs went out of use with the introduction of Buddhism in A.D. 552. Cremation became standard, and artifacts were no longer interred with the dead.

The second Tomb Period ceramic tradition, Haji Ware (*hajiki*), was entirely indigenous and developed directly out of the late Yayoi pottery tradition. Haji Ware was made by the same clay-workers' guilds (*hajibe*) who manufactured *haniwa,* the large clay figures (Fig. 8) placed on top of major tomb mounds during the Tomb Period. Like *haniwa,* Haji Ware vessels were made of plain, unglazed, porous, reddish buff earthenware. Haji was an entirely utilitarian ware; since none was deposited in tombs, surviving examples are extremely rare.

The term *haniwa* (literally "clay circles") refers either to the earthenware cylinders of the figures themselves or to the fact that they were placed in rows around the shoulders of tomb mounds. *Haniwa* range in height from about two feet to four feet. The figures are composed of hollow, basically cylindrical parts, the lower portion designed to be inserted in the slope of the burial mound. Representational *haniwa* depict persons (warriors, shamans, court ladies, musicians, peasants), animals (horses, dogs [Fig. 8], pigs, deer, birds), or objects (weapons, ritual implements, boats, houses).

Haniwa were slab-built of reddish buff earthenware and fired in wood-burning kilns. Some received painted decoration after firing. Vast quantities were produced and several areas in the Yamato region were deforested to provide wood for the kilns. Emperor Nintoku's tomb alone had twenty thousand *haniwa.* Although not all tombs used these figures, the more than ten thousand known tombs have yielded great quantities of *haniwa.* The simple, clean, contemporary looking style of *haniwa* is essentially a fortuitous result of mass production. They often have admirable vigor, charm, and individuality, but there were no self-aware sculptors among their makers, only anonymous guild craftsmen.

While the tomb mounds and artifacts deposited inside them are often nearly identical to Korean prototypes, *haniwa* are a strictly indigenous product. In China and Korea, from about the fifth century B.C. onwards, figurines of wood or clay were put inside tombs as spiritual substitutes for servants and entertainers. (Confucian teachings deplored the earlier practice of slaying actual concubines and retainers who were to attend their dead master in the next world.)

Chinese and Korean tomb figures were placed inside tombs, while *haniwa* were put outside. *Haniwa* probably resulted from combining the function of interior tomb figures with that of the large stone guardians erected along the approaches to ancient Chinese and Korean tombs.

The Nihon Shoki explains the origin of *haniwa* as follows: When Emperor Suinin's uncle died, his live retainers were interred with him. Their anguished cries made the emperor sad. A famous wrestler suggested that clay substitutes be used in the future. As a reward, the wrestler was appointed head of the clay workers' guild and ordered to manufacture *haniwa*.

This edifying story must be considered apocryphal for at least two reasons. First of all, skeletal evidence of actual burial of retainers is lacking in excavated Japanese tombs. Second, *haniwa* depicting human figures were not the earliest type. Plain cylinders came first, followed by houses, next by models of artifacts, then animals, and finally people. The *haniwa* story in the Nihon Shoki reflects Confucian concepts imported with Chinese writing to Japan.

Unadorned *haniwa* cylinders were produced from the late third century onwards. At first they stood some distance apart in a row around the shoulder of a tomb mound. By the fifth century they were being placed side by side like a palisade. It has been suggested that they formed a kind of retaining wall to keep the mound from collapsing. But *haniwa* are too light and fragile for this purpose. What they actually did was form a "spirit fence," or sacred enclosure symbolically marking off the site of the tomb, like the wood sticks supporting a *shimenawa* (sacred rice-straw rope) around a Shintō sanctuary. Many of the cylindrical *haniwa* have holes that may have held a similar rope.

Archaeological evidence indicates that house models were the first type of representational *haniwa* to evolve. Most of the house models have no supporting cylinder; they were meant to be placed directly on the top of the mound, above the tomb chamber. A *haniwa* house was a "spirit trap," a residence for the deceased's soul, intended to keep his ghost from wandering among the living. *Haniwa* houses tell us much about Tomb Period architecture, just as *haniwa* human figures, specific about details in spite of their simplicity, tell us much about the clothing and artifacts found inside the tombs.

By the fifth century, *haniwa* models of artifacts were being produced. These emphasized the deceased's prestige and provided equipment for him in the spirit world, as did the actual artifacts and small funerary models of artifacts deposited inside the tombs. Swords, shields, quivers, archers' wrist-protectors, and ceremonial sun shades were prominent among *haniwa* artifact models. One well-known example depicts a boat meant to carry a soul to the spirit world.

The next *haniwa* to develop were representations of animals (Fig. 8). Dogs and barnyard animals were common, but the most important *haniwa* animals were the war horses that helped the Yamato clans to dominate the earlier peoples in Japan. *Haniwa* models of four-legged animals usually have a separate hollow cylinder for each leg, another for the body, another for the neck, and finally one for the head. These joined cylinders often manage to express remarkably successfully the essence of the animal. For all their geometric simplicity, they are somehow imbued with life. The *haniwa* dog, though only a fragment, almost seems to pant and wag his tail.

Contrary to the pious story in the Nihon Shoki, *haniwa* representations of people were the last type to develop. Warriors in armor were common; they acted as guardians of the tomb. There were also peasants, the serfs who worked the dead chieftain's land. But the majority of *haniwa* human figures represent persons who participated in the elaborate funeral entertainments, which lasted several days. The shamans, offering bearers, dancers, singers, jugglers, musicians, and comedians depicted would continue to entertain their master forever. Grouped on the tomb, they also impressed passersby with the status of the tomb's occupant.

Haniwa have wonderful directness, simplicity, vitality, and ingenuous charm. They are good examples of the sympathetic use of natural materials that is characteristic of Japanese art. No other ceramic sculpture in the world makes more appropriate use of clay as clay.

The Asuka Period A.D. 552 – 645

Although some knowledge of it must have arrived earlier, the date recorded for the introduction of Buddhism in Japan is A.D. 552. Buddhism gave Japan more than a major new religion; it brought with it much of the material culture of the advanced civilization of China. The welcome extended to Buddhism by the progressive faction at the Imperial Court was based in part on an awareness of these potential material benefits.

Korea introduced Buddhism to Japan while attempting to secure military aid. In A.D. 552 the king of Paekche, a kingdom in southwest Korea, sent Emperor Kimmei gifts, including a gilt Buddha image, temple banners, canopies, and *sūtras* (sacred texts), along with his statement that "this doctrine is amongst all doctrines the most excellent." Paekche wanted to form a military alliance with Japan against the neighboring kingdom of Silla, but no significant aid was sent, and Paekche eventually fell. Korea was unified by Silla in A.D. 668.

Shōtoku Taishi (A.D. 574–621), the great prince regent during the reign of Empress Suiko (A.D. 554–628), was the most important early patron of Japanese Buddhism. He was also a tireless advocate of Chinese culture. He sent the first official Imperial Japanese mission to the Court of the Chinese emperor in A.D. 607, thereby circumventing Korea as the bearer of Chinese culture to Japan.

Asuka is the name of the region where most of the Imperial capitals were located during the period; it is in Nara Prefecture. (In those days, for reasons of Shintō ritual purity, the capital was moved each time an emperor died.) The Asuka Period is sometimes also called the Suiko Period.

Asuka Period ceramics (Fig. 9) consist almost entirely of utilitarian Sue Ware pieces, and surviving examples are extremely rare because the practice of depositing artifacts in tombs had been discontinued. Jars on tall pedestals, sometimes with attached figurines, went out of use at the end of the Tomb Period, since they had been mainly funerary, and more functional jars and bowls became the rule in the Asuka Period. They usually have interesting random coatings of natural wood ash glaze on the jar shoulders, and the glaze often runs toward the bases in bold drips.

The Hakuhō Period A.D. 645 – 710

Hakuhō ("White Phoenix") is the name of the Era that lastec from A.D. 673 until 685, the reign of Emperor Temmu. The term Hakuhō is used by extension for the period from A.D. 645, the year of the Taika Reforms, which attempted to restructure the government along Chinese lines, to A.D. 710, when the first permanent Japanese capital was founded at Nara. The Hakuhō Period is also sometimes called the Early Nara Period; many cultural trends that reached maturity in the Nara Period (A.D. 710–794) began in Hakuhō, but the capital at Nara had not yet been established.

During the Hakuhō Period, direct contact with T'ang Dynasty (A.D. 618–907) China became common, and Korea's role as transmitter of Chinese culture was gradually eliminated. Improved ships and better navigation made travel to China more feasible. Although Chinese influence became more and more evident in Japanese art, ceramics is generally a conservative art form, and the utilitarian Sue Ware tradition continued more or less unchanged from Asuka times (see Fig. 9). It was not until the Nara Period tha some of the splendors of T'ang ceramics made an impact on Japanese wares.

The Nara Period A.D. 710–794

The Nara Period is named after the city of Nara (then called Heijō-kyō), where the first permanent Japanese capital city was established. It is also called the Tempyō Period after an Era in the reign of Emperor Shōmu. Throughout the period, the Imperial Court and the great Buddhist monasteries made every effort to emulate the magnificent cultural achievements of T'ang China. The former Shintō practice of moving the capital when the emperor died was un-Chinese and precluded the construction of a capital worthy of the dignity of the increasingly powerful Imperial Court.

In A.D. 710 the Japanese began laying out Heijō-kyō in the grand manner of Ch'ang-an, the T'ang capital, but many blocks in the huge rectangular grid of broad avenues were never occupied. The modern town of Nara, where Japanese and foreign tourists come to visit ancient temples, occupies but a fraction of the ancient city.

The *Shōsōin* in Nara is a special log storehouse built to house the possessions of Emperor Shōmu. His widow, Empress Kōmyō, donated her husband's possessions to the great Imperial monastery, Tōdaiji, in A.D. 756. Fortunately, the building and its contents have escaped destruction. The latter are priceless and often unique eighth-century luxury goods. Included among them are Japanese imitations of T'ang objects, actual T'ang imports, and even pieces from Sasanian Dynasty (A.D. 224–642) Persia. Many of the objects are examples of things that have not survived anywhere else. Had these splendid objects perished, we would know little about Nara Period secular art.

An entirely new tradition of lead-glazed earthenware came to Japan from T'ang Dynasty China in the Nara Period. Lead oxide was included in the glaze as a flux that would cause silica to fuse at low, earthenware firing temperatures. Various metal oxides served as glaze coloring agents. Blue, green, yellow, amber, and clear glazes were used singly or in combinations. On so-called splash-glazed ware, glazes were applied in informal, irregular patches that tended to run or drip, giving the decoration a bold, spontaneous quality that puts these pieces among the most aesthetically satisfying ceramic art in the world. Most frequently, a combination of three contrasting glazes was used, hence the term *sansai* ("three-color") ware.

T'ang ceramic forms were enriched by influence from Sasanian Persian metalwork, ceramics, and glass. T'ang (and, by extension, Nara) ceramic shapes have a classic perfection that combines strength and fullness with grace and movement, just as in the best T'ang and Nara sculpture.

Sue Ware (Fig. 9) continued to be the work horse, as seen in some Shōsōin medicine jars with covers.

The Early Heian Period A.D. 794–897

The Early Heian Period is named after Heian-kyō (modern Kyoto), the new city to which the Imperial capital was transferred in A.D. 794. The period ended in A.D. 897, the year Japan decided to sever diplomatic relations with China, which was in turmoil.

The Japanese government decided that the best way to disentangle itself from the powerful Buddhist sects in Nara was to move away from the city. The effort and expense of transferring the capital underscore the urgency of escaping from the interference of the Buddhist church. Three hundred thousand peasants were pressed into service and an entire year's taxation spent on the move. Two recently introduced Buddhist sects (Tendai, introduced from China in A.D. 805, and Shingon, introduced in A.D. 806) were awarded Imperial patronage as a buffer against the older sects at Nara. The new capital city was given the name Heian-kyō (Capital of Peace and Tranquility).

Little need be said about Early Heian ceramics. Sue Ware continued to be the standard type. Since it was mainly utilitarian, few examples have survived. There was also a monochrome green-glazed ware that derived from T'ang-style green-glazed earthenware of the Nara Period.

The Fujiwara Period A.D. 897—1185

The Fujiwara Period is named after the powerful Fujiwara family, whose members were the de facto rulers of Japan at the time. By the tenth century, their clan was so firmly in control of the Court that each crown prince, generation after generation, was required to marry a Fujiwara lady. Many emperors were forced to abdicate before reaching maturity; Fujiwara regents and ministers ran the government.

The Fujiwara Period began in A.D. 897, when Japan stopped sending official embassies to China. Throughout the period, Japanese culture turned inward, assimilating earlier Chinese borrowings and creating new styles that were characteristically Japanese.

The Court had little interest in its responsibility to govern. Members of the nobility were preoccupied with Court activities such as dress, ceremony, romantic love, poetry, and incense guessing or moon viewing. The *Tale of Genji,* a novel written just after the year 1000 by Lady Murasaki, provides fascinating insight into the decadent, exquisite life of the Fujiwara Court. The common people, when mentioned at all, are spoken of like animals. Administration outside Kyoto was delegated to often corrupt governors, warriors, and sheriffs. Poverty and disorder prevailed in the provinces.

This situation could not last indefinitely, and the courtiers sensed it. There was thus an urgency about their pursuit of frivolous pleasures, a feeling for the beautiful sadness of things (*mono-no-aware*). According to Buddhist teachings, the world was going through a final, degenerate stage before its destruction and eventual rebirth.

Toward the middle of the twelfth century, misrule, aggravated by famine, caused a revolt near the capital. The Imperial Court was powerless to stop it. Members of the palace guard wore swords and arrows as emblems of office but had little skill in using them. Warriors from the northeastern provinces, called in to suppress the revolt, subsequently took control of the government and put an end to the Fujiwara Period.

During the Fujiwara Period, Japanese ceramics, along with other arts, assumed distinctly native characteristics. Sue Ware, which in the Tomb Period had been almost indistinguishable from its Silla prototype, had taken on T'ang-derived shapes in the Nara and Early Heian Periods. Sue continued to be the standard Japanese ceramic ware throughout most of the Fujiwara Period.

Japanese kilns in the Fujiwara Period were converting from the reduction firing (limited oxygen in the kiln) that produced the grays and blacks of Sue Ware to the oxidation firing that produced the buff, brown, and reddish colors of the medieval wares.

By the eleventh century, large storage jars (Fig. 12) appeared that had a characteristically Japanese look and did not show direct Korean or T'ang Chinese influence. They were used for storing grain, water, wine, or other products. The Japanese jar shape was slightly taller and more irregular than its ultimate T'ang prototype, and its lip was more prominent. The old coiling method of construction was used instead of the potter's wheel. Storage jars were often too big to be thrown in one piece but could be thrown in two pieces and joined, a common practice in China and Korea. The Japanese, however, coil-built large jars. Partly because they were coil-built and partly because of rather hasty manufacturing methods, these Japanese storage jars were nearly always somewhat irregular in form. This informality provides a warmth and visual interest often lacking in the more carefully made and mechanical looking products of the potter's wheel.

The powerfully swelling sides of the jars give them sculptural presence, which is enhanced by their rough surface texture (the result of not refining the clay thoroughly) and by the natural ash glaze that runs down their sides in long drips. The pale, glassy, green ash glaze forms the perfect complement to the rough, warm brown clay surface.

The storage jars were agricultural, commercial, and household utilitarian objects, manufactured as quickly and as cheaply as possible. It would have seemed absurd to their makers that they are now considered works of art. But Japanese tea masters of the late sixteenth century saw in these rugged, unselfconscious pots an embodiment of the highest realm of beauty. Contemporary taste verifies this judgment.

The Kamakura Period 1185–1334

The Kamakura Period is named after the coastal town of Kamakura (near modern Yokohama), where Minamoto Yoritomo established his dictatorship in 1185. Formerly a muddy fishing village, Kamakura was in the northeastern provinces far from Kyoto, within the territory controlled by the Minamoto clan before it was ordered, along with the Taira clan, to quell the revolt near Kyoto. After stamping out the rebellion, the Minamoto warriors fought the Taira warriors for supremacy from 1156 to 1185. The Minamoto eventually won, and Yoritomo had the emperor appoint him *shōgun* ("commanding general," actually military dictator). Yoritomo ruled Japan through a feudal system of warrior vassals, while the emperor remained a powerless puppet in Kyoto. Yoritomo's heirs lacked his ruthless brilliance, and control of the government was gradually usurped by the Hōjō family, supposedly loyal Minamoto retainers, who ruled through the office of *shōgun*'s regent.

Japan continued to refrain from sending official envoys to China, but many Buddhist monks went there for study. Kiyomori, head of the Taira clan during its brief period of supremacy, sent his own trading ships to China. The Hōjō regents also sent merchant ships, but the venture ended in 1274 when Kublai Khan, having already conquered China, dispatched an armada from Korea to conquer Japan. After a few initial skirmishes, the Mongol fleet was destroyed by a severe storm which the Japanese subsequently called *kamikaze* ("divine wind"). A second *kamikaze* broke up the second Mongol invasion fleet in 1281.

The courtly delicacy, refinement, and poetic allusions of Fujiwara Period art did not interest the hereditary warriors who now found themselves the rulers and new art patrons of Japan. They demanded art that was bold, direct, and realistic.

Ceramic production flourished during the Kamakura Period. A variety of characteristically Japanese wares developed at groups of kilns that had previously produced Sue Ware. It is customary to speak of the major ceramic traditions among them as the Six Old Kilns.

The changeover from Sue-type wares to the newer ones was accomplished when the kilns were converted from reduction firing to oxidation firing. Reduction limits the amount of oxygen in the kiln during firing; oxidation provides an abundance of oxygen in the kiln. The appearance of the resulting ware is quite different. Incompletely oxidized metal oxides in the clay of a reduction-fired piece yield colors ranging from gray to black, as in Sue Ware. More completely oxidized metal oxides in oxidation-fired ware yield colors in the buff to red to brown range.

Two of the Six Old Kiln ceramic types were already in production during the late Fujiwara Period. One was Tokoname (or Tokonabe) Ware, made at kilns located in Owari Province (Modern Aichi Prefecture). Tokoname Ware consisted mainly of storage jars (Fig. 10) and wine bottles (Fig. 11). The output of the Tokoname kilns was enormous, several times more than that of the more famous Seto kilns, and it continued throughout the Edo Period (1603–1868). Tokoname clay burned to a reddish tan color on the surface of the pot, but the clay body of all these medieval wares remained gray beneath the surface, as can be seen on a broken piece. There was usually a greenish or mottled yellowish deposit of ash glaze on the shoulder or side of a Tokoname pot.

The other late Fujiwara ware among the Six Old Kilns was Echizen Ware, made in Echizen Province (Modern Fukui Prefecture). Storage jars were the most frequent type. Echizen clay burned more gray-black than Tokoname, and the ash glaze turned light blue in places. Production of Echizen Ware continued into the Muromachi Period (1392–1568).

The Shigaraki Ware kilns in Ōmi Province (modern Shiga Prefecture) were among the Six Old Kilns that converted from Sue-type wares during the Kamakura Period (see Fig. 12). Production has continued to the present. Shigaraki Ware, consisting mainly of storage jars, has a wonderfully gritty surface texture caused by gravel, burst air pockets, and beads of fused feldspar in its poorly refined clay. Although it resulted at first from hasty manufacturing methods, this distinctive coarse texture came to be greatly admired by tea masters in the sixteenth century, and many pieces were commissioned specifically for tea ceremony use. The patches of cool, greenish ash glaze on Shigaraki jars form the perfect complement to its warm, reddish buff clay.

Iga Ware is not traditionally counted among the Six Old Kilns, but its background is similar. The Iga kilns too originally produced Sue-type wares. Iga storage jars are closely related to those of nearby Shigaraki but have heavier deposits of ash glaze due to longer and higher firing. From the late sixteenth century on, many flower vases and fresh-water jars (Fig. 13) for the tea ceremony were ordered from Iga potters and were especially prized by tea devotees. Iga production died down in the seventeenth century but has been revived.

The Tamba kilns were also among those of the Six Old Kilns to convert from Sue-type production in the Kamakura Period. They are located in Tamba Province (modern Hyōgō Prefecture) and are still operating. Tamba Ware (Fig. 14) has a much smoother surface, resulting from better refined clay, and a darker, reddish brown color.

Bizen Ware, produced in Bizen Province (modern Okayama Prefecture), another of the Six Old Kilns, is still in production today. Bizen Ware (Fig. 15) has a distinctive purplish brown clay surface enlivened by fire markings (*yōhen,* "kiln changes," or *higawari,* "fire changes," irregular patches of buff, red, gray, and brown surface color resulting from the uneven contact of fire on the clay). Bizen Ware ash glaze tends to pull into little yellowish droplets (*goma-gusuri,* "sesame-seed glaze").

Of all the Six Old Kilns, Seto Ware (Fig. 16) made in Owari Province (modern Aichi Prefecture, near Nagoya), was the most varied. So large was the output of the Seto kilns (the region is still one of Japan's major ceramics-producing areas) that *seto-mono* ("Seto thing") has become the most common Japanese word for ceramics, regardless of where they are made.

It is said that a potter, Katō Shirōzaemon Kagemasa, called Tōshirō, a retainer of the feudal lord Kuga Michichika, traveled to China in 1223. Tōshirō is said to have studied ceramic techniques in China and to have established kilns at Seto following his return to Japan in 1228. Some specialists accept this story, while others consider it apocryphal.

Whatever the truth, one type of Seto Ware was an imitation of Chinese Sung Dynasty celadon porcelain, and another (Fig. 16) was a copy of Sung Chien Ware (so-called *temmoku*) and other iron-oxide brown-black glazed ware. The imitations failed to duplicate their prototypes, but they had distinct merits of their own.

Kamakura Period ceramic technique was still relatively primitive compared to that of Sung Dynasty China (960–1279). The Chinese had already achieved true porcelain by the Six Dynasties Period (A.D. 220–581). The Koreans learned this ceramic technique from the Chinese by the tenth century. In spite of frequent contact with both China and Korea, Japan made no porcelain until the early seventeenth century, when a large deposit of porcelain clay was finally discovered in Kyūshū. But Kamakura Period kilns were not able to reach the high firing temperatures needed for porcelain. Seto potters tried to imitate celadon with a greenish ash glaze that is thin and glassy looking by comparison.

Chien Ware, made in China's Fukien Province during the Southern Sung Dynasty (1127–1279), consisted entirely of bowls for drinking green tea. Seto potters imitated the streaky black Chien Ware glaze and other iron-black Sung glazes with a caramel-brown glaze (Fig. 16).

The Nambokuchō Period 1334–1392

Nambokuchō means "Northern and Southern Courts." Two separate Imperial lines now claimed legitimacy, one in Kyoto (the Northern Court), the other at Yoshino (the Southern Court, in the mountains south of Nara). Each had its supporters among the feudal lords, and the succession dispute was not settled until 1392.

The Nambokuchō Period saw the ascent of Sung-style ink-monochrome painting in Japan, but there were no major developments in architecture, sculpture, or ceramics. The Six Old Kilns continued producing largely utilitarian wares, mainly storage jars, wine bottles, and bowls.

The Muromachi Period 1392–1568

A warrior named Ashikaga Takauji had himself appointed *shōgun* in 1338 and moved his headquarters from Kamakura to Kyoto. His family held the title of *shōgun* until 1568, but were never really in control of all of Japan. They were sometimes the pawns of their more powerful vassals, and civil war was frequent throughout the period.

In 1378 Yoshimitsu, third Ashikaga *shōgun*, built his palace in the Muromachi district of Kyoto. History condemns him as an "aesthete *shōgun*" who neglected government to pursue such refined pastimes as art collecting, poetry, and Nō drama. However, much of his power to govern had already been usurped by his retainers, so he had little choice in the matter. Yoshimitsu's enthusiasm for Chinese trade and Chinese culture was such that he renewed the formal tributary relations with China that had been severed in A.D. 897. He collected Chinese paintings and ceramics and liked to wear Chinese clothes and have himself transported in a Chinese palanquin.

Yoshimasa, the eighth Ashikaga *shōgun* (1435–1490), followed in Yoshimitsu's footsteps as an "aesthete shō*gun*," art collector, and poet. He was the first great patron of the tea ceremony. Meanwhile, near anarchy prevailed in the country. The common people suffered endlessly, and famine and epidemic aggravated the effects of misrule and civil war. The Ōnin War (1467–1477) marked the beginning of more than a hundred years of constant internal turmoil known as the Sengoku Jidai (Period of the Nation at War, 1467–1573).

Japan's chaos had a significant cultural side effect. Since Kyoto was nearly destroyed in the fighting, artists, craftsmen, and scholar-monks fled to other parts of Japan, dispersing culture throughout the country. The cultural attainments of the *daimyō*, the military feudal lords who governed the provinces, began to rival those of the *shōgun* in Kyoto.

During the Muromachi Period, the Six Old Kilns continued producing utilitarian wares, but interesting developments again began to take place in Japanese ceramics due to changing tastes in the tea ceremony.

The semiritual drinking of tea in Ch'an (Zen) monasteries of Sung Dynasty China as a medicinal beverage and mild stimulant to aid meditation had been brought to Japan by Zen monks returning from study in China during the thirteenth to fifteenth centuries. The tea ceremony is ultimately a Japanese secularization and formalization of this practice.

A host, who may be a professional tea master, and a small number of guests, as few as one and normally not more than four, drink tea in an atmosphere of tranquility and simple but profound aesthetic beauty. The tea is prepared one serving at a time, using the same tea bowl (*chawan*; Fig. 18). The host removes a small amount of powdered green tea (*matcha*) from the tea caddy (*cha-ire*; Fig. 17) with a thin bamboo scoop (*chashaku*). He places the tea in the tea bowl, adds water drawn from the kettle with a bamboo dipper (*hishaku*), then beats the mixture to a souplike consistency with a bamboo whisk (*chasen*). The fresh-water jar (*mizusashi*; Fig. 13) holds cool water to replenish the kettle. Each guest eats a small, sweet bean cake before drinking his tea. The ceremony is sometimes accompanied by an exquisitely served meal (*kaiseki*). After each guest has drunk the frothy green tea and admired the bowl, he returns it to the host, who rinses it with boiling water from the iron kettle (*kama*), wipes it dry, and prepares a serving for the next guest.

The tea ceremony is performed in a tiny, unelaborate room (*chashitsu*) built of ordinary natural materials impeccably designed and crafted. There is an alcove (*tokonoma*) for the display of a small painting or calligraphy scroll as well as an abbreviated flower arrangement. The little garden (*roji*) just outside the tea house is not seen from inside but is carefully laid out and maintained by the tea master to maximize its aesthetic impact and put the guests' spirits in harmony as they approach the tea house for the ceremony.

Ashikaga Yoshimasa's tea master, Murata Jukō (1422–1502), and others began to select and use simple Japanese-made utensils along with or in place of the elaborate and expensive Chinese porcelain and lacquer formerly in vogue. Small Shigaraki Ware storage jars were selected for use as flower-holders (*hana-ire*) in tea-ceremony rooms. Bizen Ware jars were adapted as tea-ceremony water jars.

This new preference inevitably led to the creation of Japanese ceramic objects specifically for tea-ceremony use. By the end of the Muromachi Period, tea masters were commissioning Bizen potters to make tea-ceremony utensils. Seto kilns made tea caddies patterned after the little brown-black glazed Ming ointment jars that had already been adapted as containers for the powdered tea. But the full development of Japanese tea-ceremony ceramics was to take place in the following period, Momoyama.

The Momoyama Period 1568–1603

The Momoyama Period was only thirty-five years long, but it was a highly significant period, both politically and culturally. Along with castles, tea houses, and gold screen painting, it saw the greatest creative flowering of ceramic art the world has ever known.

Oda Nobunaga (1534–1582), *daimyō* of the Nagoya region, tried to consolidate all Japan under his rule and is remembered as the first of the Three Great Unifiers of Japan. He captured Kyoto in 1568 and installed a member of the Ashikaga family as puppet *shōgun,* then deposed him in 1573. Nobunaga built the first Japanese castle, in the year 1576, at Azuchi near Lake Biwa north of Kyoto. Azuchi Castle was destroyed in 1582 and Nobunaga was murdered by one of his vassals.

The second Great Unifier, Toyotomi Hideyoshi (1536–1598), built a castle in 1594 at Fushimi a few miles south of Kyoto. The castle was subsequently destroyed and peach trees planted on the hill, which came to be called Momoyama ("Peach Hill") instead of Fushimi.

Nobunaga was a *samurai,* a member of the military aristocracy, but Hideyoshi was a mere farmer's son who became a foot soldier in Nobunaga's army and rose by sheer cunning to be his top general. Hideyoshi avenged Nobunaga's death and took control of Japan himself. By 1590 he had succeeded in unifying the country.

Having no more worlds to conquer at home, Hideyoshi dispatched his armies on an absurd adventure, the conquest of China. They began by invading Korea in 1592 but were eventually stopped by Korean forces. A second invasion attempt was made in 1597. Upon Hideyoshi's death in 1598, his troops returned home.

The Korean invasions had a tremendous impact on the history of Japanese ceramics. Prior to the invasions, Japanese tea masters had begun selecting certain types of coarse Korean rice bowls for use as tea bowls, arousing a considerable Japanese interest in Korean ceramics. During the invasions, whole villages of Korean potters were brought to Japan. They established various kilns in Kyūshū and southwestern Honshū. Hideyoshi himself was avidly interested in the tea ceremony, in which he was guided by the greatest tea master of all, Sen-no-Rikyū (1520–1591). Hideyoshi's interest encouraged that of other military lords, and the Momoyama Period became the golden age of tea-ceremony ceramics.

In the Momoyama Period, many old kilns converted part of their production to tea-ceremony utensils. Thus, when Tsutsui Sadatsugu became lord of Iga Province in 1584, he ordered the Iga kilns to make flower-holders (*hana-ire*), water-jars (*mizusashi*; Fig. 13), and incense containers (*kōgo*) for the tea ceremony. By the early seventeenth century, the Iga potters had completely abandoned the production of the large storage jars that had been their mainstay and were making tea wares exclusively.

Many ceramics made for tea-ceremony use are intentionally irregular or distorted. Because of modern abstract ceramic sculpture, we now take for granted these asymmetrical, irregular forms in clay. However, one must remember that in the Far East in the late sixteenth century, the concept of a ceramic vessel being intentionally distorted out of its symmetrical, wheel-thrown shape was altogether new. It was a unique result of the tea-ceremony aesthetic formulated by Sen-no-Rikyū and other tea masters, an aesthetic in keeping with the Japanese love of nature and admiration for the effects of wear and age.

Along with their large output of more utilitarian wares, the Seto kilns continued producing tea caddies (Fig. 17) and tea bowls for the tea ceremony. The caddies were patterned after little imported Ming ointment jars fitted with turned ivory lids and used to hold the small amount of powdered green tea necessary for a tea ceremony. The tea bowls were imitations of Southern Sung Chien Ware (*temmoku*) tea bowls. Both the caddies and the bowls usually had a mottled brown-black iron-oxide *temmoku* glaze.

The Shigaraki kilns produced a few *mizusashi, hana-ire,* and *chawan* during the Momoyama Period, along with their traditional storage jars. The Bizen kilns likewise devoted part of their production to tea ware, becoming noted for flower-holders, water-jars, wine flasks, and large, traylike serving plates. Many Bizen pieces made for the tea ceremony employ a unique decorative technique called *hidasuki* (see Fig. 71). *Hi* means "fire" and *dasuki* is from *tasuki,* meaning "sleeve cord," the silk cord used by Japanese women to tie back the pendant sleeves of their *kimono* while cooking or cleaning house. A few stalks of straw soaked in salt water were flung onto the surface of a pot before firing. Being wet, the straw refused to burn at first but eventually dried and burned off. Sodium in the salt water induced streaks of glazelike kiln flash and darker color where the stalks of straw had been.

Raku (Fig. 18), the most characteristic tea-ceremony ware, was not the result of modifying a portion of the production at an established kiln; it was created solely for tea ceremony use.

Sen-no-Rikyū admired the coarse, direct, unpretentious qualities of ornamental, lion-shaped roof tiles made by

Chōjirō, an immigrant Korean potter working in Kyoto. Under Rikyū's direction, Chōjirō created the first Raku tea bowl sometime during the Tenshō Era (1573–1591). *Raku* means "pleasure." Sōkei, a pupil of the first hereditary Raku potter, was presented with a seal bearing the ideogram *raku* by Toyotomi Hideyoshi in admiration of his work. From that time on, Raku potters and their imitators have usually impressed circular *raku* seals on the bottoms of their tea bowls.

Except for a few glazed pottery incense-burners (*kōro*), mostly sculpted in the form of *karashishi* (mythical Chinese lion-dogs), Raku Ware consisted almost entirely of tea bowls. Raku is low-fired earthenware with a lead glaze derived from those of Ming Dynasty China. The glaze contains lead oxide, which acts as a flux, causing the glaze to fuse at a low firing temperature. The glaze is thickly and unevenly applied, and may be either glossy or matte. The most typical Raku bowl is black, but red ones are also common (Fig. 18), and there is a rare white variety. The color, whether black or red, comes from iron oxide. A Raku bowl allowed to cool slowly in the normal way turns red as the iron in the glaze fully oxidizes. The black is obtained by quickly removing the still-hot bowl from the hot kiln with iron tongs and smothering it in water or ashes. Iron in the glaze only partially oxidizes, producing the desired black color, called *hikidashiguro*, "pulled-out black."

Some Raku tea bowls are thrown on the potter's wheel, while others are built by coiling or pinching. The intentionally uneven shape and irregular surface is roughly formed with the hands and then finished with a trimming tool. The thick, uneven glaze application produces further subtle variations of form and texture. A good Raku tea bowl is a piece of abstract ceramic sculpture to be enjoyed by holding and feeling as well as looking. The ware has remained a noted Kyoto product; the potter Raku Kichizaemon (born 1932) is the fourteenth generation from Chōjirō.

Other Korean potters migrating to Japan in the sixteenth century established more than two hundred kilns producing Karatsu Ware near Karatsu City in Hizen Province (modern Saga Prefecture), northern Kyūshū. One rare dated Karatsu jar has an incised inscription bearing a date equivalent to 1582, but most of the Karatsu kilns were founded by Koreans who came to Japan as a result of Hideyoshi's invasions in 1592 and 1597.

Karatsu Ware shapes, glazes, and decoration are extremely close to certain early Yi Dynasty (1392–1910) Korean wares. Karatsu clay burns to a rich, warm brown on the exposed surfaces, whose torn texture results from quick, bold trimming. The most typical Karatsu glaze is gray, either glossy or matte, either crackled or uncrackled. E-garatsu (Picture Karatsu) has underglaze designs painted in iron-oxide brown-black (Fig. 19).

A few tea bowls, flower holders, and *mizusashi* were made at some of the Karatsu kilns, but except for *mukōzuke*, most of the production was more utilitarian. *Mukōzuke* are small bowls in sets of five for use in the formal meal accompanying an extended tea ceremony. Karatsu Ware continued to be made throughout the Edo Period. Nakazato Tarōemon, who was born in 1895 and is called Muan, is a twelfth generation Karatsu potter (see Fig. 72).

Satsuma Ware (Figs. 20 and 21) and Yatsushiro Ware (Figs. 22 and 23) were also first made in Japan by Korean potters brought there as a result of Hideyoshi's invasions at the end of the sixteenth century. Satsuma Ware was made in Satsuma Province (modern Kagoshima Prefecture), Kyūshū. The Satsuma Ware that concerns us here is not to be confused with the dreadful export ware of the same name that flooded the markets of Europe, England, and America in the late nineteenth and early twentieth centuries. Called "brocaded" Satsuma, the export ware was a cream-colored, glazed earthenware with vulgarly profuse and sometimes coarse decoration in overglaze enamel colors and gold. Its popularity in the West was so widespread that "Satsuma," even more than "Imari," became a household word. "Brocaded" Satsuma was first made about 1795 for Japanese use, with somewhat more care and restraint than the later export versions. After the reopening of Japan to the outside world in the middle of the nineteenth century, it became a hot export item, mass-produced in Kyoto and Yokohama as well as Satsuma.

The original type of Satsuma Ware, made from the end of the sixteenth century onwards, was usually stoneware with a thick, rich, black or brown glaze, or a combination of the two, sometimes mottled with a little white or yellow (Fig. 20). Some of the pieces were utilitarian, others were made for the tea ceremony. In both taste and purpose, this Satsuma Ware stands at virtually the opposite aesthetic pole from the later "brocaded" Satsuma.

Yatsushiro Ware was made in Yatsushiro County, Higo Province (modern Kumamoto Prefecture), Kyūshū, from 1632 onwards. It consisted mainly of tea ceremony ware for the Hosokawa *daimyōs*. Yatsushiro Ware potters make a specialty of the Korean-derived technique of slip inlay called *mishima* (see Fig. 22). Designs are stamped or incised in the surface of the leather-hard clay, and a coating of white slip (liquid clay) is painted on. After the slip dries, the excess is wiped off, exposing the design "inlaid" with white clay in the surrounding gray clay. The whole is then covered with a semitransparent glaze. Many Yatsushiro pieces are decorated with stamped inlaid motifs closely related to Korean prototypes of the early Yi Dynasty (fifteenth–sixteenth centuries), such as rope patterns and stylized chrysanthemum-like blossoms.

Shino (Figs. 24 and 25) and Oribe (Figs. 26 and 27), two other great Momoyama Period ceramic traditions, developed in central Honshū, independent of Korean influence. Although the finest pieces were made for the tea ceremony, they represented an entirely different taste from the *wabi-sabi* austerity of Raku or the robust coarseness of Karatsu. Innovative tea masters in the generation after Sen-no-Rikyū, notably Furuta Oribe (1544–1615), reacted against Rikyū's austere style and introduced brighter color and bolder decoration into tea-ceremony ceramics.

Ki Seto and Seto-guro were made in Mino Province (modern Gifu Prefecture). They are grouped together with Shino and Oribe Ware under the general heading of Mino Ware. Mino Province became an important ceramic production center during the Momoyama Period when potters fled there from the Seto area to escape the civil wars. Under the direction of Kyoto tea masters, they began producing new types of ceramics for the tea ceremony.

The names of Ki Seto Ware and Seto-guro Ware are confusing. Ki Seto (Yellow Seto) Ware was made at Mino, not Seto; the same is true of Seto-guro (Seto Black) Ware. But until 1930, when the great contemporary Shino potter Arakawa Toyozō (see Fig. 70) discovered sherds and the site of one of the Mino kilns, the Mino wares were thought to have been made at Seto. Ki Seto Ware consists mainly of tea bowls, deep serving plates, incense burners, and incense boxes. They have a thin, dry, yellowish glaze, often with simple incised decoration enhanced by a small splash of green glaze. Ki Seto is extremely rare and was produced only during the Momoyama Period, as was Seto-guro, which is even rarer and consists entirely of black-glazed tea bowls.

Shino and Oribe continued to be manufactured in the early Edo Period, but the best pieces were all made during the late sixteenth and early seventeenth centuries. Shino Ware has a thick, rich, white, feldspar glaze that often shrinks or crawls, which means it pulls away from the clay in places during firing (see Fig. 24). There are three varieties of Shino Ware, each utilizing the white glaze in a different manner. The most typical is E-shino (Picture Shino), in which underglaze iron painted decoration appears as a deep wine red through the translucent white glaze (see Figs. 24 and 25). In Nezumi-shino (Gray Shino), overall reddish iron-oxide slip is seen as gray through the thick white glaze. In Red Shino, the rarest type, the glaze application is thinner so that the iron-bearing slip appears brownish orange rather than gray through the glaze.

Oribe Ware is named after the famous tea master Furuta Oribe, under whose direction it was originally developed. Oribe was a *samurai* and became a general in the armies of Oda Nobunaga and Toyotomi Hideyoshi. He studied tea ceremony under Sen-no-Rikyū, but found Rikyū's style too austere for his taste and eventually created his own style. The bright, bold underglaze iron painted designs, cream-colored ground, and the one corner dipped in luscious green glaze characteristic of Oribe Ware display Furuta Oribe's preference for more dynamic and colorful effects than those advocated by Rikyū.

The Edo Period 1603–1868

Tokugawa Ieyasu (1542–1616), third of the Three Great Unifiers of Japan, succeeded where his two predecessors had failed; he founded a shogunate that lasted for over two hundred fifty years, a remarkably long period of stability in a country so frequently torn by civil war. The Edo Period is named after Edo (modern Tokyo), where Ieyasu established the seat of his rule. The Emperor remained a ceremonial puppet in Kyoto, living on an allowance doled out by the shogunate.

The Edo (Tokugawa) Period's opening date is usually given as 1603, the year Ieyasu had the emperor bestow on him the title of *shōgun*, but is sometimes given as 1615, the year Ieyasu destroyed Hideyoshi's son and heir in the battle of Osaka Castle, thus eliminating any challenge to his supremacy.

Ieyasu built himself a great castle at the town of Edo in the center of his former *daimyō* domain. Completed in 1606, Edo Castle was even more extensive than Osaka Castle. The sprawling grounds of the present Imperial Palace in Tokyo, with their sloping, high stone walls and wide moats, are vestiges of the inner circle of defenses at Edo Castle.

Ieyasu set up a system of totalitarian feudal rule to insure the continuing succession of his heirs, who, even more conservative than Ieyasu, attempted to freeze Japanese society. Men were obligated to do the same work as their fathers. Travel was restricted. *Daimyō* had to spend half of each year in Edo under the surveillance of the secret police. During his alternate half year in his home province, a *daimyō* had to leave his wife and son in Edo as hostages.

At first, Ieyasu tolerated Portuguese, Spanish, Dutch, and English missionaries and merchants, hoping to gain access to Western technology and trade. But eventually he began to view Christianity as a threat to his regime. In 1612 he began enforcing anti-Christian edicts, and most of the missionaries and foreign merchants were deported. In 1616, European ships were prohibited from all ports except Nagasaki and Hirado in southern Kyūshū. By 1639 all foreigners except the Dutch and Chinese were excluded from Japan. The Chinese were confined to Nagasaki and the Dutch to their trading station on Deshima Island in Nagasaki harbor. Japanese were forbidden to travel abroad.

In spite of all the restrictions, however, the Edo Period saw the rise of the merchant class. By the late sixteenth century, rich merchants were becoming important patrons of the arts.

The most significant development in ceramics during the Edo Period was the manufacture of porcelain (Fig. 28). In 1616, Ri Sambei, a naturalized Korean, discovered a large deposit of porcelain clay at Izumiyama near the town of Arita in Hizen Province (modern Saga Prefecture), Kyūshū. Sambei was one of the potters brought to Japan by armies returning from Hideyoshi's invasions of Korea. He settled in Kyūshū and made Karatsu Ware before his discovery of the porcelain clay bed at Izumiyama. After his discovery, he established a porcelain kiln at Tengudani, near Arita. Within fifteen years, most of the other kilns in the vicinity had converted production from Karatsu Ware to blue-and-white porcelain.

Porcelain clay has a high kaolin content that permits it to withstand the high firing temperatures (around 1300 degrees Celsius) necessary to vitrify porcelain. (The European definition of porcelain as a translucent ceramic ware does not apply to Far Eastern porcelain, which usually has an opaque body. The Far Eastern definition merely requires that the ware be resonant.)

Early Arita porcelain goes by various names: Arita Ware, after the town near which it was made, Imari Ware, after the port from which it was shipped to other parts of Japan, including Nagasaki, where vast quantities were traded to the Dutch for export to Europe, and Hizen Ware, after the province in which it was made. Ko-Imari (Old Imari) or Shoki Imari (Beginning-period Imari) distinguish it from eighteenth century and later Imari porcelain (Fig. 33).

The first use of overglaze-enamel color decoration on porcelain in Japan is traditionally ascribed to a potter named Sakaida Kakiemon. He is said to have developed enamel decoration in 1643 and to have died in 1666, but all this may be mere legend. Kakiemon potters produced overglaze-enamel porcelain (Figs. 34 and 35) throughout the second half of the seventeenth century and still make it today. The story of Sakaida Kakiemon may be an attempt to claim that they were the first in Japan to use enamel decoration. At any rate, by the middle of the seventeenth century, many of the kilns around Arita were producing overglaze-enamel porcelain as well as blue-and-white, a white porcelain with a transparent glaze over underglaze decoration painted in a cobalt-oxide blue (Fig. 28).

Enameled porcelain first appeared in China late in the Sung Dynasty and was popular throughout the Ming and Ch'ing Dynasties. Enamel is simply low-fired colored glaze. A porcelain piece was first biscuit fired at a medium temperature. Then the cobalt blue was painted on (overglaze enamels were usually used in conjunction with underglaze blue). Next the clear glaze was applied, after which the piece was subjected to high temperature porcelain firing. Then the colored enamels were painted on and the piece was fired again at a low temperature to fuse the enamel to the surface of the glaze. If gold leaf was added, the piece had to be fired a fourth time at a still lower temperature in order to fuse the gold leaf to the enamels and the glaze.

Kakiemon Ware (Fig. 35) has a distinctive delicacy and crispness in its enamel designs. A vast number of other Arita-area kilns produced a wide variety of enameled porcelain styles classified as Imari Ware (Figs. 31–33). The prefix *Ko* ("old") is used to distinguish the earlier pieces.

The Nabeshima Clan were the *daimyō* of Hizen Province. They established "house kilns" on their estates to manufacture porcelain for exclusive clan use and as gifts to other *daimyō* and the *shōgun* (see Fig. 36). Although production began in 1628, Nabeshima Ware was not made commercially before the Meiji Period (1868–1912). It is the most technically perfect Japanese porcelain; pieces with even minute flaws were destroyed. The enameled porcelain for which Nabeshima Ware is best known was at its finest between 1688 and 1735.

Ko-Kutani ("Old Kutani" to distinguish it from imitations made after the kilns were revived in 1823) is technically crude when compared to Nabeshima. But the boldness of its designs makes Ko-Kutani Ware by far the most striking Japanese porcelain (Figs. 37 and 38). Ko-Kutani was produced from about 1650 to about 1690; the kilns went out of business because of financial problems throughout Kaga Province. Yoshidaya Denemon re-established the kilns in 1823 (see Fig. 39). The nineteenth-century pieces are fairly uninspired imitations of the seventeenth-century ones.

The Ko-Kutani kiln sites with their telltale sherds have yet to be discovered, despite years of diligent searching by ceramic scholars. Wide variations in the technical properties of the pieces now classified as Ko-Kutani make it probable that they were produced in several different places. Some of them were almost certainly made near Arita. Nevertheless, tradition ascribes the manufacture of Ko-Kutani to Kutani Village in Kaga Province (modern Ishikawa Prefecture), on the coast of the Japan Sea in central Honshū, far from the porcelain kilns of Kyūshū. The nineteenth-century revival of Kutani took place there.

Tradition says that a man named Goto Saijirō discovered a deposit of porcelain clay in Kaga Province while supervising work at a gold mine and that Maeda Toshiharu, *daimyō* of Kaga, sent him to Arita to master porcelain manufacturing techniques. Upon his return, Saijirō established a porcelain kiln at Kutani Village.

Nonomura Ninsei (died about 1660) is Japan's single most famous potter (see Fig. 40). He was the first to use overglaze enamel decoration on earthenware as opposed to porcelain. His design motifs were derived from the paintings and decorative arts of Japan, unlike the designs on most Arita Ware, which were inspired by Chinese porcelain.

A flourishing enameled earthenware industry arose in Kyoto from the work of Ninsei. Kiyomizu Ware (named after the famous Kyoto temple near the kilns) is the best known of several wares grouped together as Kyō (Kyoto) Ware (Figs. 41–43).

Ninsei's work also laid the foundation for the career of another brilliant artist-potter, Ogata Kenzan (1663–1743), younger brother of the great painter Ogata Kōrin (see Figs. 44 and 45).

About 1682, while living at Takagamine, an artists' colony founded by Honnami Kōetsu, Kenzan studied ceramics under Honnami Kōho, Kōetsu's grandson. Kenzan received his inheritance in 1687. He moved into a Kyoto house near the Ninnaji Temple in 1689 and lived in partial seclusion while devoting himself to the study of literature, calligraphy, painting, and pottery-making. It was here that he came under the influence of Ninsei's work.

In 1699 Kenzan established a kiln of his own at Narutake, a suburb northeast of Kyoto, and began to use Kenzan as his art name. He produced enameled earthenware with highly creative designs related to the paintings of Sōtatsu and Kōrin as well as the calligraphy, lacquer, and pottery of Kōetsu.

Among Kenzan's most striking creations are cream-colored earthenware pieces with powerful, spontaneous, sophisticated designs painted in iron-oxide brown-black under a clear glaze. On several of these, Kōrin collaborated with his younger brother; after Kenzan fashioned the piece and signed it on the back, Kōrin painted a design on the front and signed it (see Fig. 44).

By 1712 Kenzan had squandered his considerable inheritance and had to rely on pottery-making, which had been his hobby, for a livelihood. He was forced to rent his kiln at Narutake to other potters and move back into Kyoto. He opened a pottery shop on Second Avenue (Nijō), where he made and sold ceramics of a more commercial variety. In 1737 he moved briefly to the town of Sano in Shimotsuke Province (modern Tochigi Prefecture).

Folk Ceramics

The term *mingei* ("folk art") was not coined until about 1918. Prior to that, pottery-making, and even the work of painters, sculptors, and architects, was considered a trade rather than an art. The whole concept of the fine arts did not exist in Japan before the Meiji Restoration of 1868 and the influx of Western ideas. The words *bijutsu* ("art") and *geijutsu* ("the fine arts") were invented in the early 1870s.

Among the various categories into which the modern Japanese divide their old ceramics (archaeological, medieval, tea-ceremony, etc.) is one for folk ceramics. This category includes mainly somewhat roughly made, boldly decorated Edo Period stoneware originally intended for everyday use by ordinary people. Characteristic types were made at various kilns in Kyūshū, Seto, and Mino.

The big seventeenth-century Mino-Kasahara Ware serving bowls (Fig. 46) were produced at some of the same Mino kilns that made Oribe Ware for the tea ceremony. Instead of having one corner dipped in green glaze like Oribe pieces, these bowls have a thin trail of the green glaze dripped randomly around the interior just inside the lip. The center is filled with a "millet stalk" (actually pampas grass) design painted in iron brown-black on a cream-gray or tan ground. The motif is rendered with such spontaneous vigor that it becomes very nearly an abstraction.

Among the most striking folk ceramics are the large Futagawa Ware kneading bowls (Fig. 47) and wide-mouthed jars made at Yumino, Hizen Province (modern Saga Prefecture), Kyūshū, in the eighteenth and nineteenth centuries. They almost always have a bold pine tree design in overglaze iron-brown and copper green on a ground of *hakeme* (white slip painted with a wide, flat brush) and a finger-combed wave pattern in the white slip on the exterior.

Three classic types of Japanese folk pottery were made at Seto kilns in the Late Edo Period (early nineteenth century): *aburazara, ishizara,* and *uma-no-me sara.* (*Sara* means "plate" or "dish.") *Aburazara* ("oil plates," also called *andonzara,* "lantern plates") are round, flat dishes with upturned rims (Fig. 48). Such a dish was placed in the bottom of a wood-framed, paper-covered *andon* ("oil lantern") to catch any hot oil that might drip from the wick of the little oil lamp in the upper part of the lantern lest it set fire to the paper housing and the surrounding *tatami* mats. Earlier *aburazara* had been made out of metal, but ceramic ones came into vogue in the early nineteenth century. The characteristic Seto type has a lively, simple, iron-brown painted design made up of landscapes, flowers, or bamboo. Sometimes one corner is dipped in green glaze, Oribe style. *Ishizara* (literally "stone plates," perhaps because of their hefty, thick walls) are big, shallow serving bowls used for herring stew and other things (Fig. 49). Made at Seto, they usually have wonderfully free paintings of flowers or birds in iron-brown and cobalt-blue.

Uma-no-me means "horse eye," a concentric-circle motif resembling a bull's-eye but oval rather than round (the round kind is called *ja-no-me,* "snake eye"). Five or six such motifs painted in iron-brown form a continuous border around the undecorated central zone of each Seto horse-eye plate for a very handsome and contemporary looking design (see Fig. 50).

Modern Japan

Meiji Period 1868–1912 | Taishō Period 1912–1926 | Shōwa Period 1926–present

By the mid-nineteenth century, Europe and America had already experienced the industrial revolution. But Japan was still a feudal country, having undergone few basic changes since the beginning of the seventeenth century. The status quo was successfully maintained by the arch-conservative Tokugawa shogunate, whose isolation policy kept Japan closed to the outside world for two-hundred-fifty years. Mid-nineteenth century *samurai* still wore two swords tucked through their belts, just as their forebears had done since the sixteenth century. Their soldiers were still armed with matchlock muskets exactly like those first copied from Portuguese ones in the mid-sixteenth century. Mid-nineteenth century Japanese were still forbidden to travel abroad. Except for the Dutch and Chinese in Nagasaki, foreigners were not permitted in Japan. Yet there were no effective coastal defenses to keep foreigners out. Japan's feudal leaders did not adequately perceive the advances in European and American shipbuilding and armament.

In 1853 Commodore Matthew C. Perry was sent from America to Japan with a fleet of sail-and-steam warships. He arrived at Uraga in Sagami Province (modern Kanagawa Prefecture) and presented the *shōgun*, Tokugawa Ieyoshi (1793–1853), with a letter from President Millard Fillmore demanding that Japanese ports be opened to foreign ships for water and supplies. Perry departed after informing the shogunate that he would return the following year for an answer. He sailed to Japan again with seven warships in 1854 and held a month-long series of talks with Japanese officials. A provisional treaty was signed opening two Japanese ports to American ships.

Similar treaties were soon negotiated by England, Russia, and Holland. Ports were opened, foreign settlements with consulates established, and trade carried on at Shimoda, Yokohama, Kobe, Nagasaki, and on Hokkaidō. The lack of protective controls in the treaties caused serious economic problems in Japan. Domestic prices went up drastically because goods were exported in such quantities that shortages developed at home. Cheap manufactured goods imported from industrialized countries were sold in Japan for much less than their hand-made equivalents, decreasing demand for Japanese products and lowering employment.

Dissatisfaction with the government became widespread. The humiliating realization that Japan was now at the mercy of "foreign barbarians" whose modern ships and weapons allowed them to impose their will on a helpless nation served to crystallize the desire to topple the Tokugawa regime.

The shogunate fell and was followed by the Meiji Restoration, the return of administative power to the emperor. "Meiji" is the posthumous name of the young emperor to whom rule was restored.

Meiji Tennō (1852–1912), known as Mutsuhito during his lifetime, was the one-hundred-twenty-second emperor of Japan. He was a man of great insight and administrative ability who carried out the crucial reforms that the Restoration put him in a position to accomplish. He became emperor in 1867 at the age of fourteen. His father, who died suddenly in 1866, had been nearly as conservative and anti-foreign as the shogunate. Mutsuhito, however, was convinced of the need for modernization. He and the clans that supported the Imperial cause realized that this could only be achieved by a strong central government.

Emperor Meiji appointed skilled advisors and issued a remarkable series of Imperial edicts to set in motion the profound social changes by which Japan became a modern nation almost overnight. In 1871 feudalism was abolished; the various provinces with their feudal fiefs were replaced by prefectures. In 1875 a senate was created, in 1885 a cabinet was formed, and in 1889 the national assembly opened.

In the cultural sphere, the first decade of the Meiji Era saw a massive influx of Western culture and a determined Japanese effort to master it. In their initial rush to catch up with the modern world, the Japanese temporarily rejected their own cultural heritage. Traditional artists and craftsmen found little demand for their work, and many had to turn to other trades. By the second decade, however, an inevitable reaction set in. Many intellectuals, statesmen, and artists asserted that it was demeaning to emulate foreign ways—Japan should build on her own great traditions. Westernization was castigated as a denial of Shintō, Buddhist, and Confucian teachings. In the arts, the earlier progress made in mastering Western styles was nearly overwhelmed by the reaffirmation of nationalism. By the third decade of the Meiji Era, the two opposing camps, pro-Western and pro-Japanese, reached a sort of equilibrium they have maintained to the present day. Within each camp have appeared many factions, quarreling among themselves, issuing manifestos, holding exhibitions, and keeping the art scene lively. The government has been directly involved in the arts and the factional disputes through its selection of curriculum and faculty at government art schools and the government-sponsored art exhibitions at home and abroad.

During the initial flurry of Westernization, there was widespread neglect of Japan's ancient cultural treasures. Priceless art objects were sold to foreigners as curios.

Buddhist temples lost patronage; buildings, statues, and paintings fell into ruin. The government edict permanently separating Shintō and Buddhism took its toll: Shintō sanctuaries in Buddhist precincts were destroyed and vice versa.

An American graduate of Harvard College, Ernest Fenollosa (1853–1908), was invited by the Japanese government in 1879 to teach philosophy at the new Tokyo Imperial University. He and his student, Okakura Kakuzō (1862–1913), were staunch advocates of traditional Japanese-style art. Together they were instrumental in the resurgence of nationalism in the arts through their teaching posts in the government schools. They contributed to a reawakening of interest in Japanese art of the past through their lectures and essays. They helped preserve Japan's cultural heritage by recommending surveys and protection of ancient art treasures. This led to the formation of the Cultural Properties Commission and the National Treasure registration laws. The Japanese had formerly regarded Buddhist paintings and sculpture simply as church furnishings and objects of worship, but Fenollosa recognized their aesthetic significance. Through him, Okakura and the Japanese people became aware of the beauty in great religious art.

Fenollosa and Okakura also did much to promote the appreciation of Japanese art abroad. In 1886 they led a delegation to America and Europe to study Western art administration and art education as well as to acquaint foreigners with the glories of Japanese art. Each of the two men was subsequently a curator of Oriental art at the Museum of Fine Arts in Boston. Okakura's books in English, such as *Ideals of the East* and *The Book of Tea,* have been very influential.

In the field of ceramics, major changes took place during the Meiji Period. It will be recalled that throughout preceding periods, ceramic production had been a local village craft: each pottery or porcelain town produced its own type of ware with its own style of decoration. The various production centers, whether large ones like Seto or small ones like Tamba, worked in relative isolation from each other. A *daimyō* whose fief contained kilns was anxious to guard his potters' technical secrets and protect his monopoly on their wares. With the abolition of feudalism in 1871, potters found much of their market and distribution system eliminated, and many were suddenly without a livelihood.

Within a few years, however, ceramics and other crafts enjoyed a revival, but on quite different terms than those before the Restoration. The rapidly expanding export trade provided a vast market for craft goods. Anxious to strengthen the economy, the government took steps to encourage craft production for the foreign market. Export wares were called *hamamono,* since Yokohama was the main port involved in the export trade.

Japan had her own industrial revolution during the years immediately following the Restoration. The Meiji government invited European and American technicians to set up Western-type factories for mass production in Japan. Dr. Gottfried Wagner, a German chemist, introduced European ceramic production methods to the Japanese. He arrived in 1868, the very year of the Restoration, and worked in various parts of Japan. In 1882 and 1884 and 1885, he built European-type commercial kilns in Tokyo, where he died in 1892.

Active Japanese participation in European and American international expositions whetted foreign appetites for Japanese goods. The earliest overseas display of Japanese wares was at the Paris Exposition in 1867. Next came the San Francisco Exposition of 1871. At the Vienna Exposition of 1873, and numerous others that followed, the Japanese exhibits were fully subsidized by the government. Officials and craftsmen were sent with the exhibits to study the Western market and learn Western manufacturing techniques. The potters Nōtomi Kaijirō (1844–1918) and Kawahara Chūjirō (1849–1889) accompanied the exhibits to the Vienna Exposition and remained in Europe to study ceramic production. Upon their return they introduced the use of plaster molds for casting ceramics.

The unexpectedly enthusiastic response of Westerners to Japanese wares at the Vienna Exposition and others helped encourage a revival of the crafts in Japan. So did the frequent purchase of outstanding craft products by the Imperial Household. At the First National Industrial Fair in Tokyo in 1877, and many subsequent domestic expositions, the arts and crafts were brought to the attention of the Japanese public (see Fig. 54).

A potter whose career epitomized the best in the ceramic art of the Meiji Period was Miyagawa Kōzan (1842–1916). Born in Kyoto and trained as a potter, Kōzan deliberately moved to Yokohama early in the Meiji Period and devoted himself to producing fine ceramics for export. His ceramic sculpture and vessels were acclaimed at the 1876 Centennial Exposition in Philadelphia, the 1893 World's Columbian Exposition in Chicago, and the 1900 Paris Exposition, among others. In 1896 he was appointed a member of the Imperial Art Academy, the highest honor bestowed on Japanese artists and craftsmen. This official recognition was a source of great encouragement, not only for Kōzan but for other potters as well.

Kōzan was one of the few Meiji potters who had both perfect technique and superb design sense. One reason his work is so satisfying is the restraint in its form and decoration. Alas, the same may not be said of most Meiji ceramics. Eager to please the Western market, Meiji potters were overwhelmed by Victorian elaboration. They abandoned the key crafts principle that form and decoration must enhance each other. Complex, realistic figural or landscape scenes were painted on the surfaces of ceramic vessels. The shapes of vessels also suffered from inconsistency and lack of restraint. Elements borrowed from European styles ranging from classical antiquity to Art Nouveau were combined willy-nilly and even mixed with traditional Chinese or Japanese forms.

One goal achieved too successfully by Meiji craftsmen in lacquer, cloisonné, and ceramics was the recreation of elaborate paintings on the surfaces of vases and boxes. These were tours de force in technique, which was at its highest level, able to accomplish nearly anything, yet ultimately self-defeating. A painting is, after all, a painting. Rendering a complex painting on a vase requires the costly expenditure of much time, effort, and technique, yet the result cannot begin to equal the original.

The Crafts Movement

Japan's rapid industrialization following the Meiji Restoration seriously threatened its long tradition of superb handmade craft products, which resulted in the temporary blurring of the distinction between crafts and industry. The word "crafts" (*kōgei*) was now extended to mean "industrial technology." The government viewed the crafts as a branch of industry and encouraged their adaptation to mass production for both the export and domestic markets.

The first new Western-style ceramics factory was built at Nagoya in 1904, based on a German prototype. In 1906 and 1907, others were constructed at Kyoto, Seto, Arita, and elsewhere. Together with Western methods of manufacture came a trend to imitate Western designs. Mass production encouraged standardization, so the unique characteristics of each district's crafts began to disappear.

Artists were called in to design craft products and supervise their decoration. Individual craftsmen no longer created their own distinctive pieces. Handmade items were gradually replaced by machine-made ones, which could be sold more cheaply. Many traditional craftsmen found no market for their wares. Age-old crafts techniques—in ceramics, weaving, dyeing, paper-making, lacquering, basketry, metalwork, etc.—were neglected and sometimes forgotten. In accordance with European practice, crafts were now regarded as inferior to art, and in their new industrialized condition, they certainly were. In 1907 government art exhibitions ceased including crafts at all.

Fortunately, a group of three dedicated potters and one brilliant aesthetician arose in time to save the crafts from oblivion. These founders of the Japanese crafts movement were the philosopher–art critic Yanagi Sōetsu (1889–1961) and the potters Bernard Leach (born 1888), Hamada Shōji (1894–1977), and Kawai Kanjirō (1890–1966).

The crafts movement in Japan was a counter–industrial revolution parallel to the Arts and Crafts Movement in England. Like John Ruskin and William Morris, Yanagi Sōetsu sought a return to the beauty of handmade objects, the greater fulfillment of the craftsmen in their production, and the greater satisfaction of the consumers in their use. The crafts movement in Japan achieved much more widespread and lasting success than its counterpart in England.

Yanagi was a remarkable man, a gifted thinker whose brilliant writings on artists and mystics of the Western world served to deepen his appreciation of the crafts in his own country and Korea. Born in Tokyo, Yanagi was educated at the Peers School and Tokyo Imperial University, where he received a degree in philosophy. He and his friends, some of whom were members of the old Kyoto court nobility who were later to become well-known writers, started a monthly magazine called *Shirakaba* (White Birch) in 1910. This journal led the field in introducing Western literature, art, and philosophy to the Japanese people. During the thirteen years of the magazine's existence, Yanagi was one of its chief editors as well as a frequent contributor. He was especially interested in the English mystic William Blake and the American poet Walt Whitman, publishing a major book on the former in 1914 and a magazine devoted to the two from 1929 to 1930.

Among his many achievements, Yanagi was a professor at Dōshisha University and lectured on Buddhist art and aesthetics at Harvard in 1928–29. He was the guiding theoretician of the Japanese crafts movement, writing voluminously on the subject. He also became the first director of the Japan Folk Art Museum.

In 1918 Yanagi invited the English potter Bernard Leach (see Fig. 55), who had just returned to Japan after two years in

Peking, to build a kiln on his family's estate at Abiko, twenty-five miles east of Tokyo. Leach, originally a painter, first came to Japan in 1909 and studied pottery-making under the sixth-generation Kenzan (he is affectionately referred to by the Japanese as "Kenzan VII"). When he started his own pottery workshop in Japan in 1912, Leach was ridiculed at first for throwing his own pots. According to the prevailing idea, throwing was done only by lowly workmen; the artist-potters simply created the designs and applied the decoration. However, serious potters throughout Japan soon joined Leach in insisting that a potter is an artist who must create his own piece from start to finish.

Leach worked at Abiko for a year and was involved in frequent discussions with Yanagi and his literary friends about the transition from local folkcrafts to industrialization and self-conscious individual artists. While considering William Morris's crafts movement in England, Yanagi realized that there was no word in the Japanese language for "folk art." The crafts, as well as painting, sculpture, and architecture, had simply been considered various trades, neither fine art nor folk art. Yanagi coined the term *mingei* ("folk art, art of the people") for the work of humble, anonymous, traditional craftsmen. He regarded it as superior because it was natural, spontaneous, and unselfconscious.

In 1919 Yanagi and Leach were joined at Abiko by the potter Hamada Shōji (see Figs. 56 and 57). While visiting the mountain monasteries on Kōya-san in 1926, Yanagi, Hamada, and the latter's potter friend, Kawai Kanjirō (see Figs. 58–62), decided to start a crafts society. They organized the Nihon Mingei Kai (Japan Folk Art Association) with Yanagi as president. In 1931 the society began publishing its splendid crafts magazine, *Kōgei,* with Yanagi as editor. In 1936 the society established the Folk Art Museum (Mingei-kan) in Tokyo with Yanagi as director.

The crafts movement has been a great success. The Folk Art Museum now has branches in Kurashiki, Tottori, Osaka, and other cities. Antique folk art is now avidly studied and collected by the Japanese and recently by foreigners as well. Modern craftsmen have revived many of the old traditions, and their wares sell briskly in *mingei* shops all over Japan, so much so that *mingei* production and marketing are now becoming somewhat commercial themselves. Fine craftsmen are now once again regarded as artists in their own right, even by the government, which awards a title popularly known as *ningen kokuhō* ("Living National Treasure") to the best of them.

Among the artists and craftsmen honored with this designation at its inception in 1955 was the potter Hamada Shōji (see Figs. 56 and 57), with whom Yanagi and Kawai founded the Japanese crafts movement. Hamada's pots have been shown frequently in England, America, and Europe. Dozens of kilns in the town of Mashiko, where Hamada lived and worked for over fifty years, turn out frank imitations of his work for sale in *mingei* shops throughout Japan. Mashiko Ware is good, honest, inexpensive pottery, but it lacks the spark of genius that infuses the master's own work. In his throwing and trimming, in the proportions of his slab-mold pieces, in his simple decoration with brush or ladle or fingers, one sees the unselfconscious directness, vigor, strength, and creative imagination of an inspired craftsman whose technical skill has long since become second nature.

Hamada's *Black-Glazed Octagonal Bottle Vase* (Fig. 57) has faceted sides cut with a potter's knife when the clay was leather-hard (the piece was thrown with extra thick walls for this purpose). The spontaneous directness of the cutting is quite remarkable. There is no decoration, but the thick iron-black *temmoku* glaze forms a perfect complement to the sculptural shape of the bottle. The facets are inspired by those of late Yi Dynasty (eighteenth and nineteenth centuries) Korean food jars, which usually have a caramel-brown iron glaze. Yi Dynasty ceramics are among the finest folk pottery in the world and have long been one of Hamada's major sources of inspiration. Okinawan pottery of the seventeenth through nineteenth centuries is another. Hamada does not merely imitate, however. Influences are assimilated and restated in personal, contemporary terms.

Hamada was born in Tokyo in 1894. He studied pottery-making under the artist-potter Itaya Hazan (1872–1963) in the Ceramics Department of the Tokyo Technical College from 1913 to 1916. One of his fellow students there was Kawai Kanjirō, who became his close friend and crafts movement co-founder. After graduation, Hamada and Kawai both became engineers at the Kyoto Ceramics Testing Institute, where they met another great modern potter, Tomimoto Kenkichi (1886–1963). Hamada and Kawai conducted a series of ten thousand glaze experiments while at the Institute.

In 1918 Hamada met Bernard Leach at an exhibition, and the two men became life-long friends. The following year Hamada joined Leach at his kiln beside Yanagi Sōetsu's house in Abiko and there met Yanagi for the first time. Later the same year Hamada and Kawai made a trip to Korea and Manchuria. When Leach returned to England in 1920,

Hamada went with him, and they built a Japanese-style climbing kiln at St. Ives in Cornwall, where Leach's home and workshop have remained until the present day. In 1923 Hamada had his first one-man exhibition, at the Paterson Gallery in London. He then set out for Japan via France, Italy, Crete, and Egypt.

Upon his return to Japan in 1924, Hamada settled in the pottery-making town of Mashiko, a three-hour train ride north of Tokyo in Tochigi Prefecture. He married Kazue Kimura and went with her to Okinawa on their wedding trip. He made pottery at the Tsuboya kiln in Okinawa in 1925 and had his first one-man show in Japan the same year. Each year since then he has had his own exhibition in Tokyo and Osaka. Leach worked with Hamada at Mashiko in 1934. Hamada traveled throughout Korea in 1936 and 1937 with Yanagi and Kawai, collecting crafts for their new Folk Art Museum. Hamada traveled throughout Europe with Yanagi in 1952 and conducted demonstration workshops in the United States with Leach the same year.

Hamada's *Square Plate with Wheat Stalk Design* (Fig. 56), made about 1960, is a characteristic example of his work. The stalk of wheat motif, painted with a few flicks of the brush, is virtually his trademark. He has done it thousands of times for more than fifty years with never a loss of energy in the brushstrokes, and of course, no two wheat stalks are exactly alike. Here the design is painted with iron-brown slip on a crawled, light gray rice-husk ash glaze within a mottled tan iron-glazed border stamped with a molded checkerboard pattern.

Hamada's close friend Kawai Kanjirō (see Figs. 58–62) had been Hamada's fellow student at Tokyo Technical College from 1913 to 1916 and fellow engineer at the Kyoto Ceramics Testing Institute after graduation. Yanagi, Hamada, and Kawai founded the Japan Folk Art Association in 1926.

Though not as well known outside Japan as Hamada, Kawai is nonetheless considered one of the greatest modern Japanese potters. He has long been famous for the originality and the variety of shapes in his slab-mold pieces (Figs. 61 and 62). Born in Shimane Prefecture, he lived in Kyoto most of his adult life. His kiln and traditional Japanese house, filled with antique Japanese and Korean furniture and crafts and his own ceramics and sculpture, is now a museum.

Kawai's early works, such as the *Brown-Glazed Tea Bowl with Wax-Resist Chevrons and Blossoms* (Fig. 58), are rather similar to Hamada's: solid, folk art–style pieces inspired by traditional Japanese and Korean ceramics. In the 1950s and 1960s, however, Kawai became more personal, innovative, and modern in his work.

During the 1950s, high-relief slip-trailed designs touched with various colored glazes were one of Kawai's specialities (Fig. 61). Earlier examples often have simple, sprightly, underglaze-painted abstract floral and geometric motifs; later ones frequently have the trailed-slip decoration. Among the glazes for which Kawai is especially well known are *gosu* (see Fig. 60), which is partially-refined cobalt-oxide blue with interesting iron-oxide brown inclusions, and *shinsha* (see Fig. 59), which is underglaze copper red.

Toward the end of his life, Kawai, tiny, thin, and frail, developed a bold, powerful new style that was thoroughly contemporary and international, yet completely his own (Fig. 62). On a ground of unglazed, orange-buff, gritty Shigaraki clay, he splashed wild blobs of the brightest red, green, black, and cream glazes, dribbled on like those in a Jackson Pollock painting.

Kitaoji Rosanjin (1883–1959) was the most eclectic of the great modern Japanese potters (see Figs. 63–69). Whereas most other potters worked within the framework of one distinct ceramic tradition (Hamada: *mingei* [Fig. 56]; Arakawa Toyozō: Shino [Fig. 70]; Kaneshige Tōyō: Bizen [Fig 71]; Nakazato Muan: Karatsu [Fig. 72]), Rosanjin tried his hand at a wide variety of traditional styles. Never slavishly imitative, he simply took inspiration from a style and created his own distinctive pieces.

Rosanjin's stylistic eclecticism, together with the fact that most of his pots were thrown by his assistants, led Hamada and others to criticize him severely. According to Hamada, Rosanjin was "not a potter, merely a decorator." While some of Rosanjin's pieces are certainly more successful than others, one can but admire the courage it took to try so many different styles, any one of which another potter would have apprenticed for years to master. And when Rosanjin was at his best, he was superb.

As for the fact that Rosanjin did not personally throw most of his pots, he nevertheless closely supervised the throwing operation and often did the final trimming and shaping himself. One should bear in mind that Bernard Leach was laughed at in 1912 for throwing his own pots.

Though a master at throwing, Hamada of course had numerous assistants who helped with all aspects of production. In spite of Hamada's contempt for Rosanjin, the prices of Rosanjin's ceramics in Japan have recently outstripped Hamada's, and Rosanjin is highly regarded abroad as well, having had a one-man exhibition at Japan House Gallery in New York City in 1972.

Rosanjin began his career as a calligrapher, a skill that was later to serve him in good stead while decorating porcelain nd stoneware dishes and vases with painted designs or alligraphy (see Fig. 63). The same type of brush is used for oth. In 1915, at the age of thirty-two, Rosanjin began two ears of study at a Kutani porcelain kiln in the city of anazawa. After that he moved to Kita-Kamakura, where he ater built a kiln of his own in order to supply appropriately rtistic ceramics for the elegant service of Japanese food in a ine restaurant of which he had become manager. But in 1936 e lost his job with the restaurant because of his legendary ad temper and turned to making ceramics full-time. He isited the United States and France in 1954.

Much of Rosanjin's ceramic output before World War II onsisted of porcelain, which took inspiration from Imari lue-and-white (Fig. 63) as well as Kutani overglaze enamel tyles (see Fig. 64). After the war, Rosanjin concentrated on toneware rather than porcelain, inspired by a multitude of raditions, including Bizen (Fig. 65), Shino (Figs. 66 and 67), ribe (Fig. 68), and Kenzan (Fig. 69).

ven from this brief survey of Japanese ceramics, it is pparent that from their inception in the late Stone Age hrough their remarkable popularity in modern Japan, eramics have played an unusually important role in the life f the Japanese people. As in the West, a ceramic vessel in apan may be merely utilitarian, or it may have an rnamental function, or often both. But only in Japan do ertain of the finest ceramics achieve recognition as *art*, ully equal to painting, sculpture, and architecture.

This Japanese respect, if not to say reverence, for good eramics has had a salutary effect on the West in recent ears. The discovery of Japanese pottery styles and echniques by modern English, Scandinavian, European, and American artist-potters has played a part in the recent esurgence of crafts in the West. Lately it has become ossible for an occasional hard-working potter in America to arn a decent living without resorting to teaching. All of us enefit from the increased availability of good hand-made bjects today. And what is perhaps most important, the apanese have taught us to appreciate the very real beauty of eramic art.

1
Earthenware Beaker
Middle Jōmon Period, *circa* 2500 B.C.
H: 35.5 cm. (14 in.).
Applied and incised decoration with cord-impressed surface pattern.
Museum Purchase 74.28.1

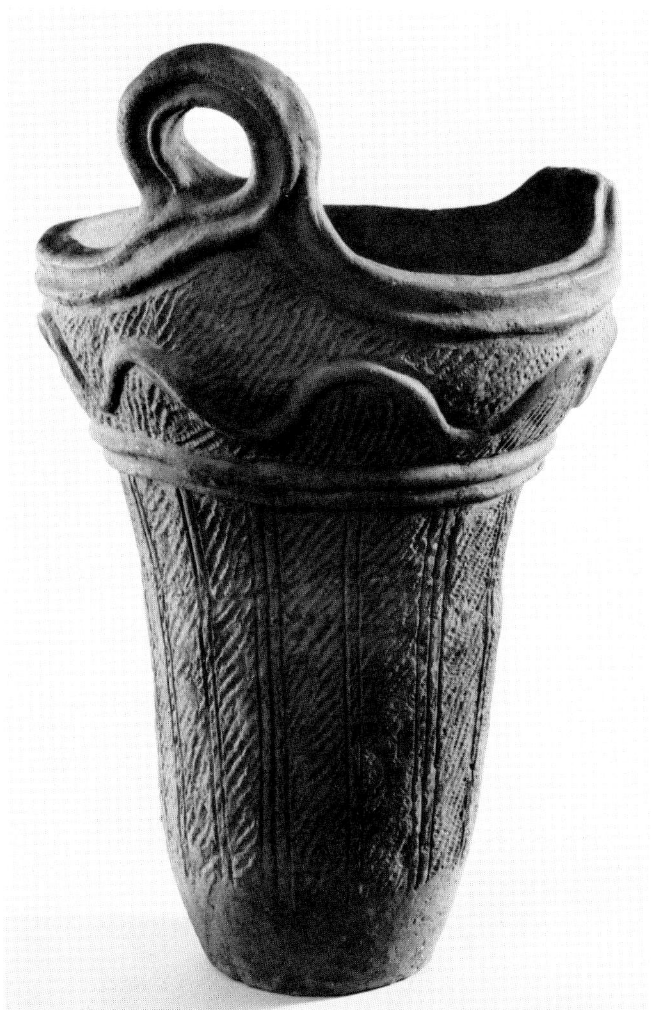

2
Earthenware Beaker
Late Jōmon Period, *circa* 1500 B.C.
H: 16.8 cm. (6⅝ in.).
Incised decoration.
Lent by Dr. and Mrs. Robert Dickes L76.16

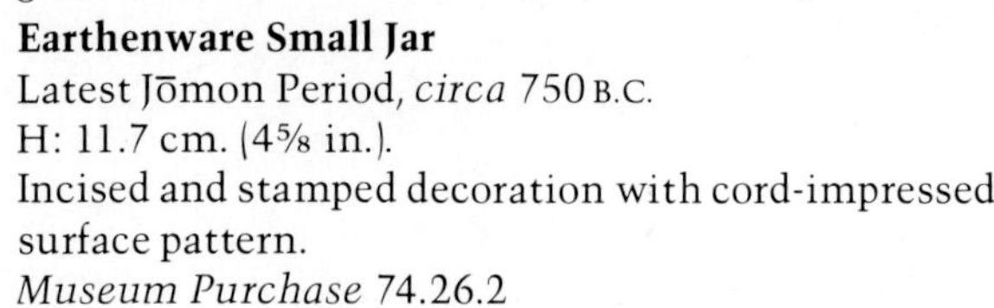
3
Earthenware Small Jar
Latest Jōmon Period, *circa* 750 B.C.
H: 11.7 cm. (4⅝ in.).
Incised and stamped decoration with cord-impressed surface pattern.
Museum Purchase 74.26.2

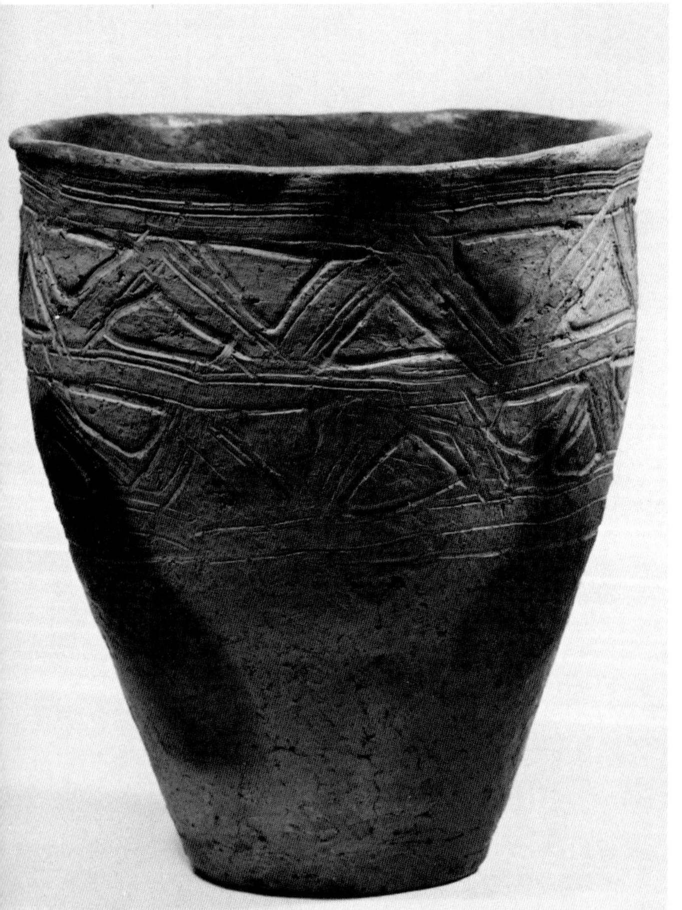

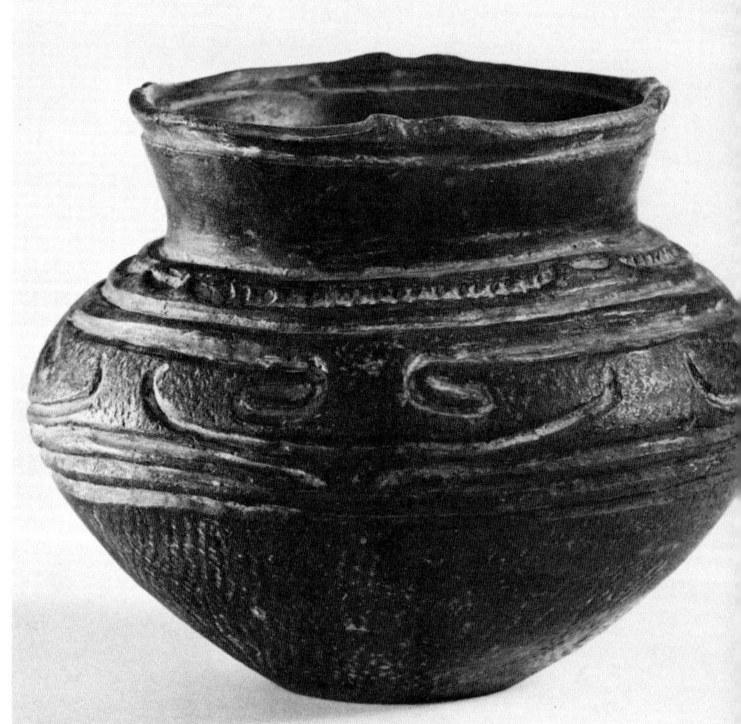

4
Earthenware Figurine (head, torso, and right arm)
Late Jōmon Period, *circa* 1500 B.C.
H: 7.6 cm. (3 in.).
Incised surface ornamentation.
Gift of Mr. and Mrs. Carl L. Selden 74.110

5
Head from an Earthenware Figurine
Latest Jōmon Period, *circa* 750 B.C.
H: 6.7 cm. (2⅝ in.).
Incised and stamped surface ornamentation.
Lent by Leighton Longhi L78.57

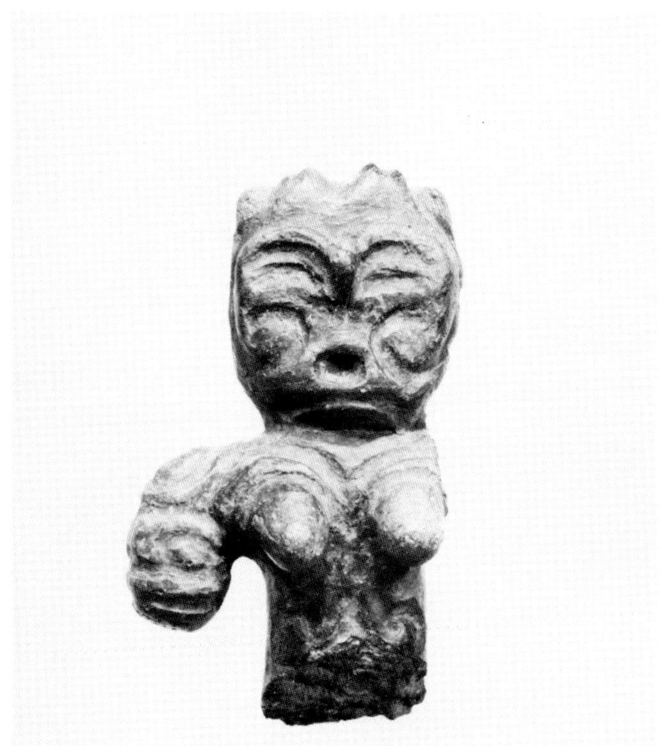

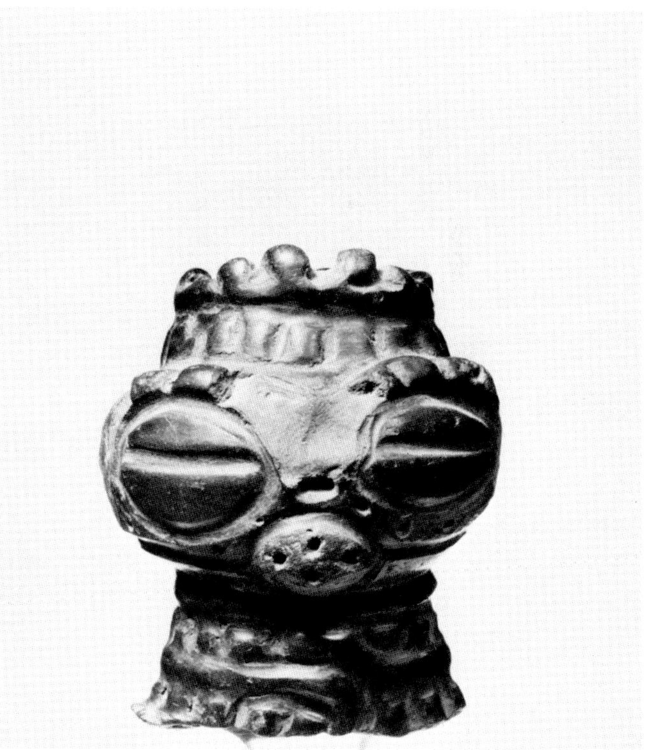

6
Earthenware Jar
Yayoi Period, *circa* 1st century A.D.
H: 27.7 cm. (10⅞ in.).
Combed surface texture, applied clay "buttons."
Gift of Carll H. De Silver 74.26.1

7
Sue Ware Jar with Attached Miniature Vessels
Tomb Period, 5th–6th century A.D.
H: 16.5 cm. (6½ in.).
Gray stoneware with combed design below lip.
Gift of Mrs. Albert H. Clayburgh in memory of her mother, Mrs. E. Evelyn Dorr 66.33

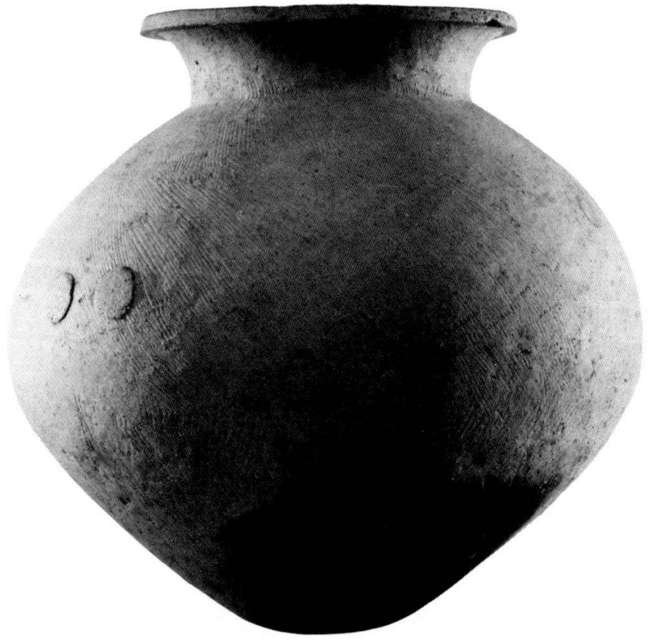

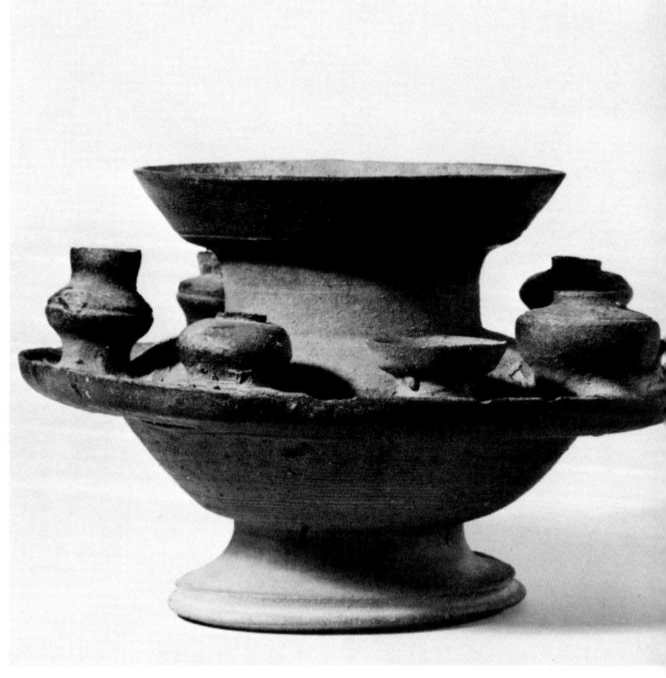

8
Haniwa Head of a Dog (fragment of a complete figure)
Tomb Period, 5th–6th century A.D.
H: 41.6 cm. (16⅜ in.).
Earthenware.
Lent by Mr. and Mrs. Carl L. Selden L78.62

9
Sue Ware Jar
Nara Period, 7th–8th century A.D.
H: 25.7 cm. (10⅛ in.).
Coil-built gray stoneware with natural ash glaze deposit.
Museum Purchase 76.118

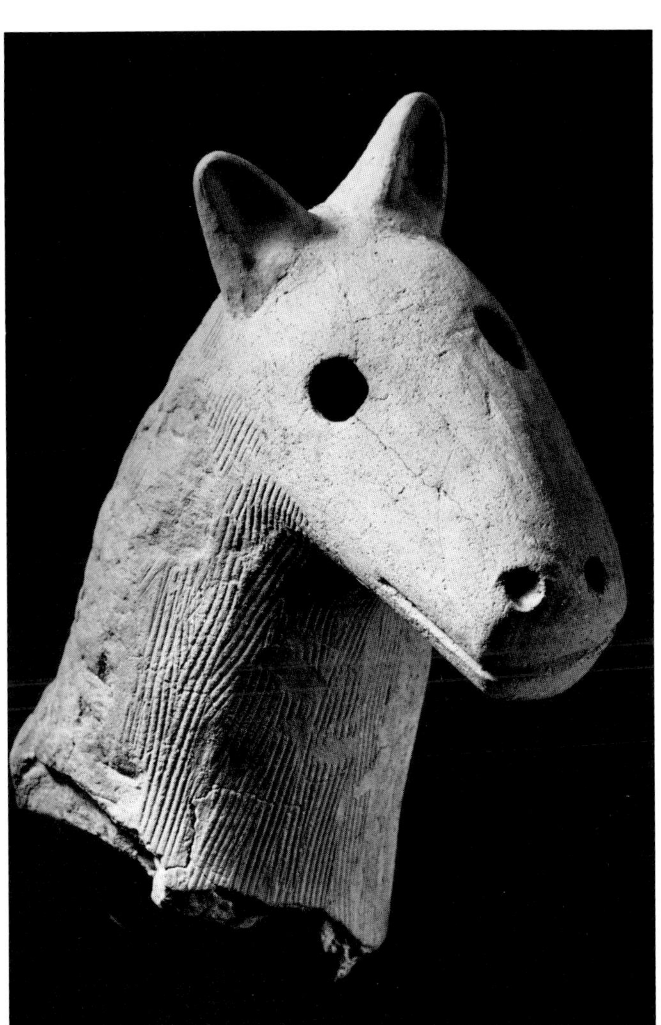

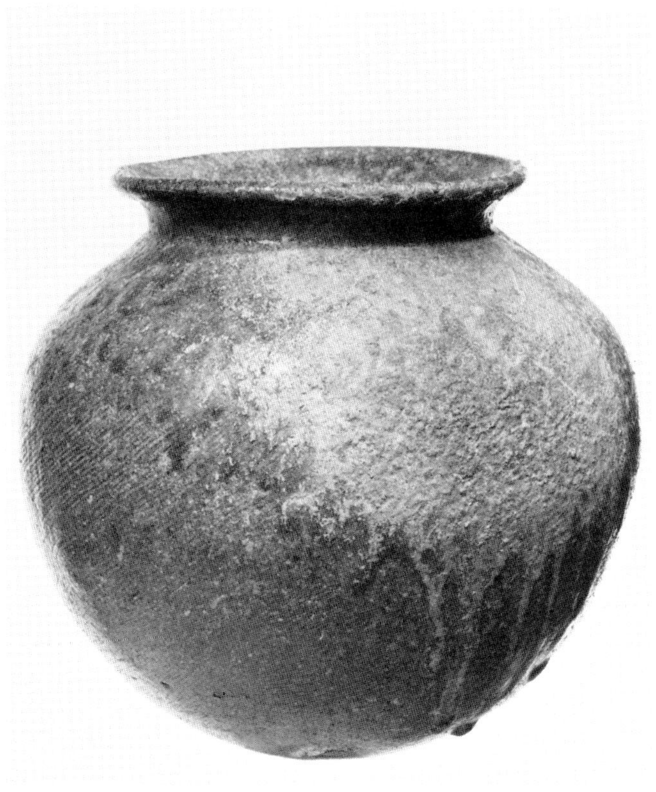

10
Tokoname Ware Storage Jar
Nambokuchō Period, 14th century.
H: 21.6 cm. (8½ in.).
Reddish brown stoneware with a deposit of natural ash glaze all over one side.
Lent by Mr. and Mrs. Joseph P. Carroll L78.67.10

11
Tokoname Ware Wine Bottle
Edo Period, 17th century.
H: 29.2 cm. (11½ in.).
Reddish brown stoneware with a deposit of natural ash glaze on the shoulder.
Lent by Mr. and Mrs. Joseph P. Carroll L78.36.3

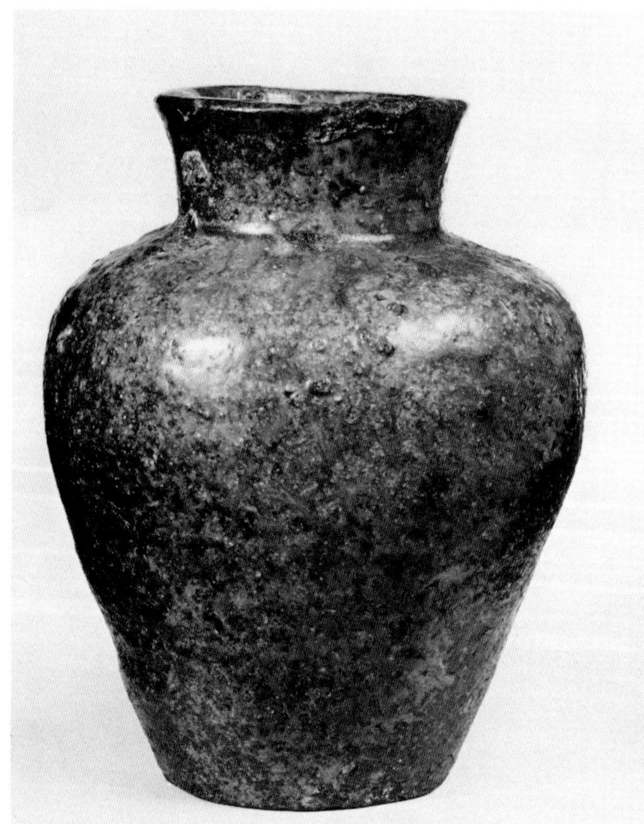

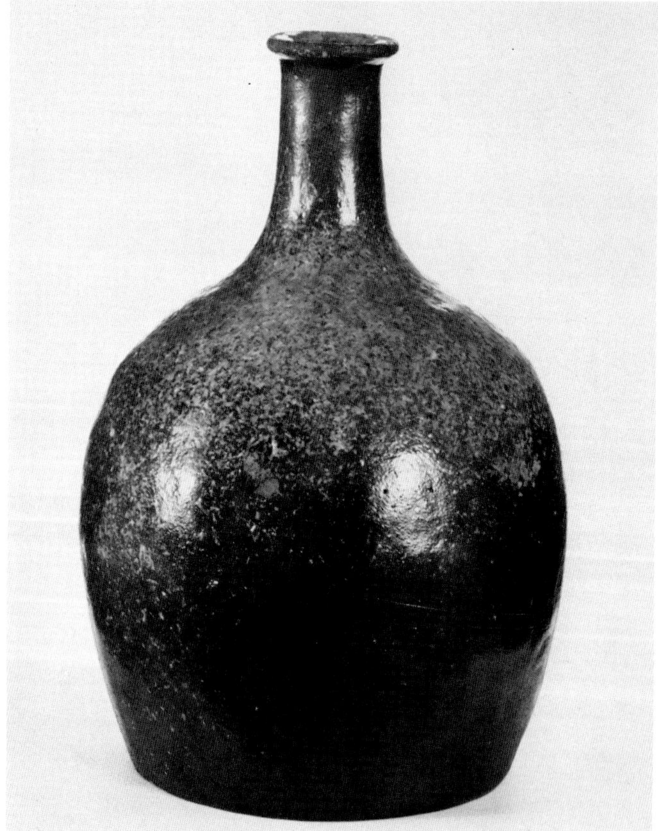

12
Shigaraki Ware Storage Jar
Nambokuchō Period, 14th century.
H: 50.8 cm. (20 in.).
Coil-built orange-buff stoneware with traces of natural ash glaze.
Babbott Fund 73.32

13
Iga Ware *Mizusashi* (Tea Ceremony Fresh Water Jar)
Momoyama Period, late 16th–early 17th century.
H: 10.5 cm. (4⅛ in.).
Buff stoneware with generous deposit of natural ash glaze all over.
Lent by Margery and Harry Kahn L78.24

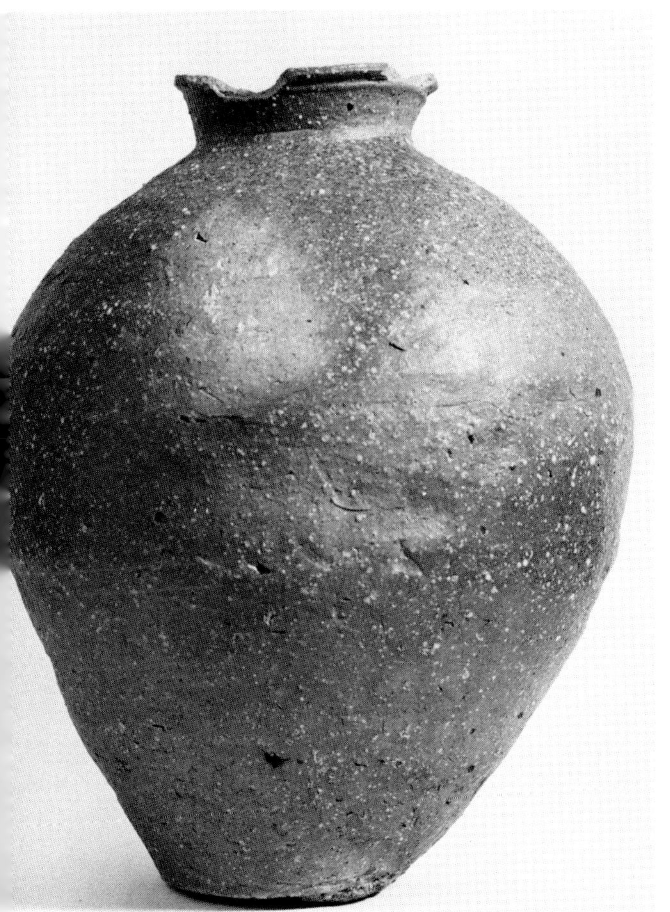

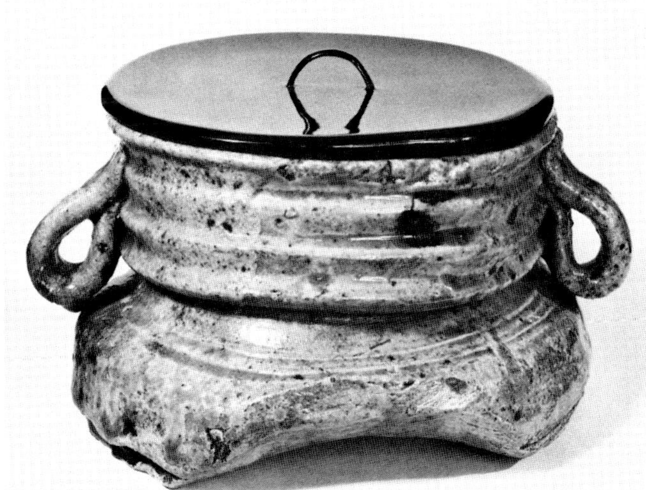

14
Tamba Ware Tea Storage Jar
Edo Period, 17th century.
H: 27.6 cm. (10⅞ in.).
Brown stoneware with applied ash glaze.
Museum Purchase 74.111

15
Bizen Ware Storage Jar
Muromachi Period, 15th century.
H: 30.5 cm. (12 in.).
Coil-built purple-brown stoneware with combed design and natural ash glaze deposit on shoulder.
Gift of David James 74.58

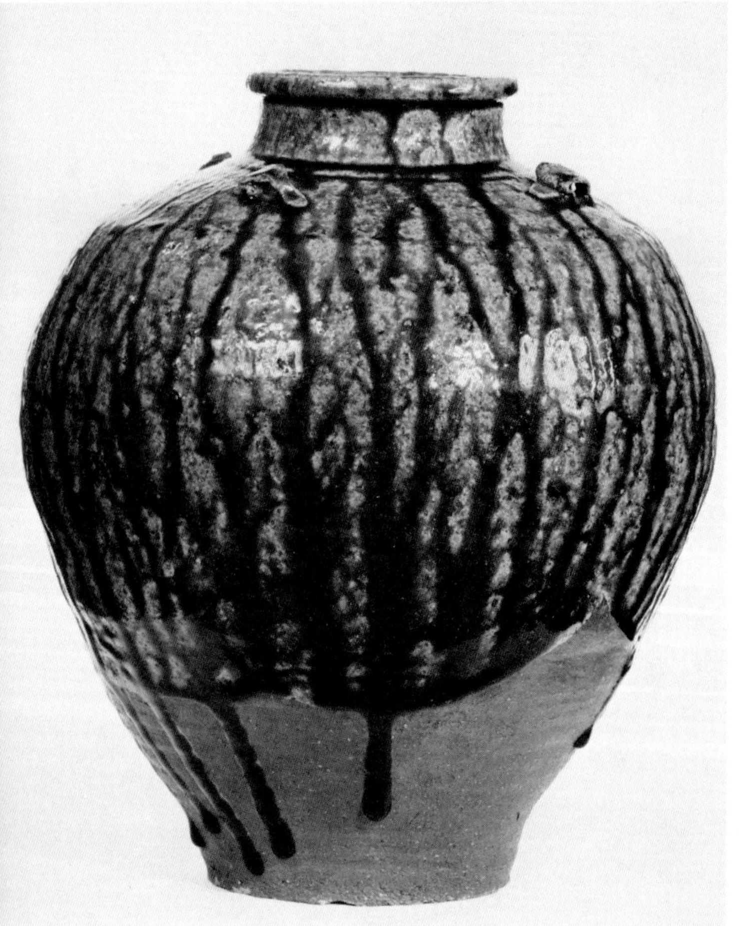

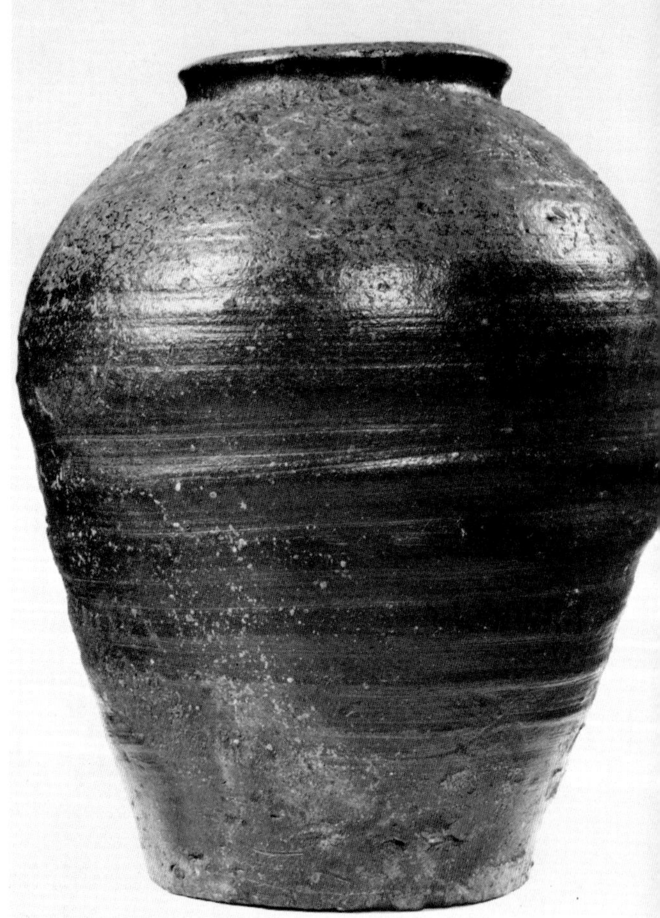

16
Ko-Seto Ware Wine Bottle
Kamakura Period, 13th century.
H: 26.1 cm. (10¼ in.).
Brown-glazed stoneware with stamped decoration of vine scrolls and flowers.
Anonymous Gift 78.204

17
Seto Ware Tea Caddy
Edo Period, 18th century.
H: 8.5 cm. (3⅜ in.).
Tan stoneware covered (except for lower portion) with brown glaze streaked with yellow glaze; ivory lid.
Gift of Robert B. Woodward 07.280

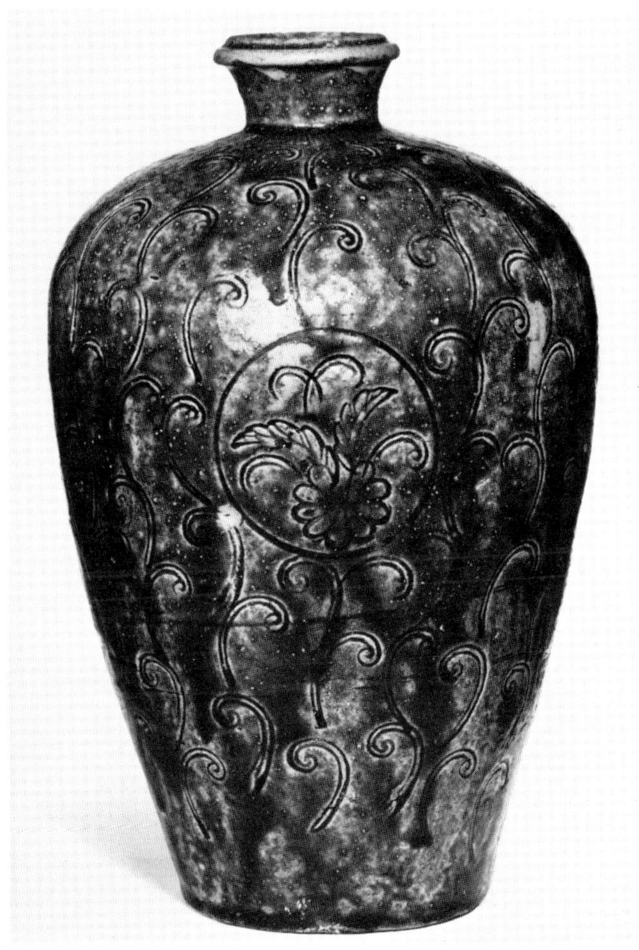

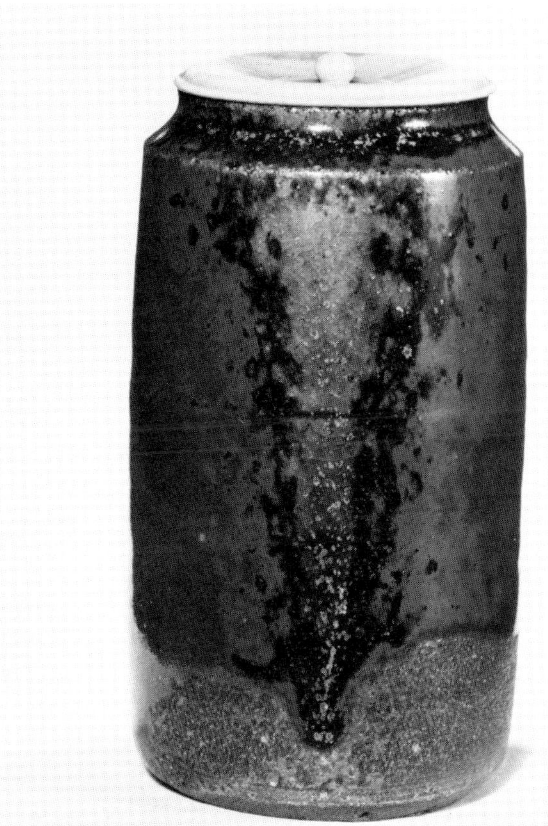

18

Red Raku Ware Tea Bowl

Edo Period, late 17th–early 18th century.
Sōnyū 1664–1716, the 5th generation Raku master
H: 7.6 cm. (3 in.).
Earthenware with an overall reddish, grayish, yellowish mottled glaze.
Gift of Mrs. Frederick B. Pratt 74.53

19

E-Karatsu Ware *Mukōzuke* (Side Dish for the Tea Ceremony Meal)

Momoyama Period, late 16th–early 17th century.
W: 14 cm. (5½ in.).
Gray-glazed stoneware with underglaze iron-black painted decoration.
Lent by Mr. and Mrs. Joseph P. Carroll L78.36.7

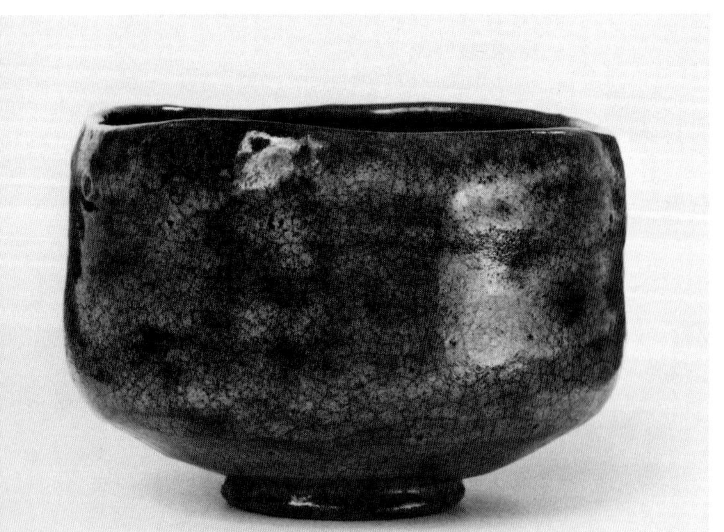

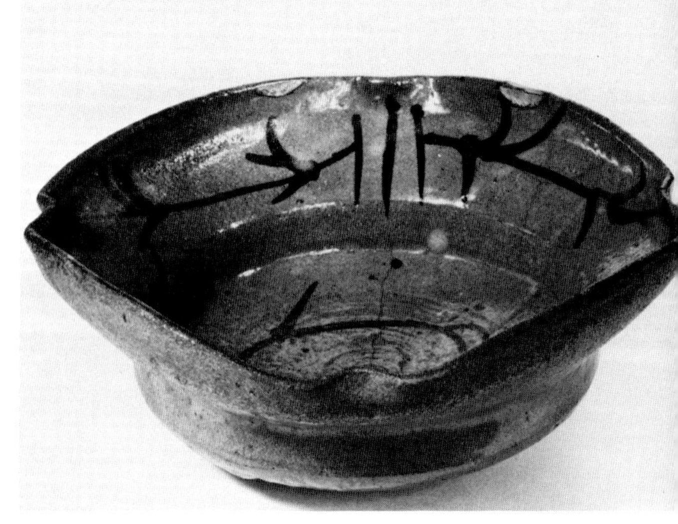

20
Satsuma Ware Tea Caddy
Edo Period, 17th–18th century.
H: 9.7 cm. (3⅞ in.).
Brown stoneware with a black glaze speckled with white; ivory lid.
Gift of Robert B. Woodward 13.41

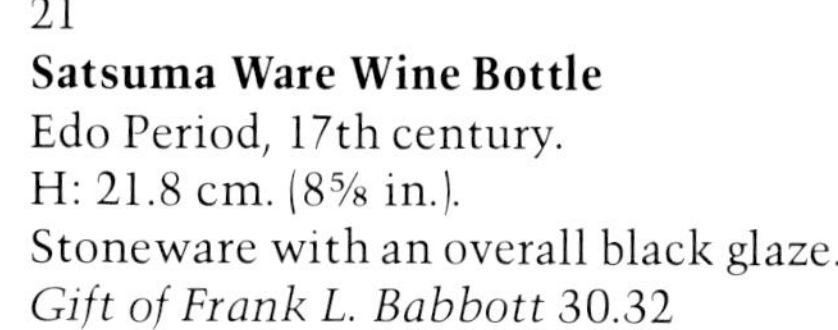

21
Satsuma Ware Wine Bottle
Edo Period, 17th century.
H: 21.8 cm. (8⅝ in.).
Stoneware with an overall black glaze.
Gift of Frank L. Babbott 30.32

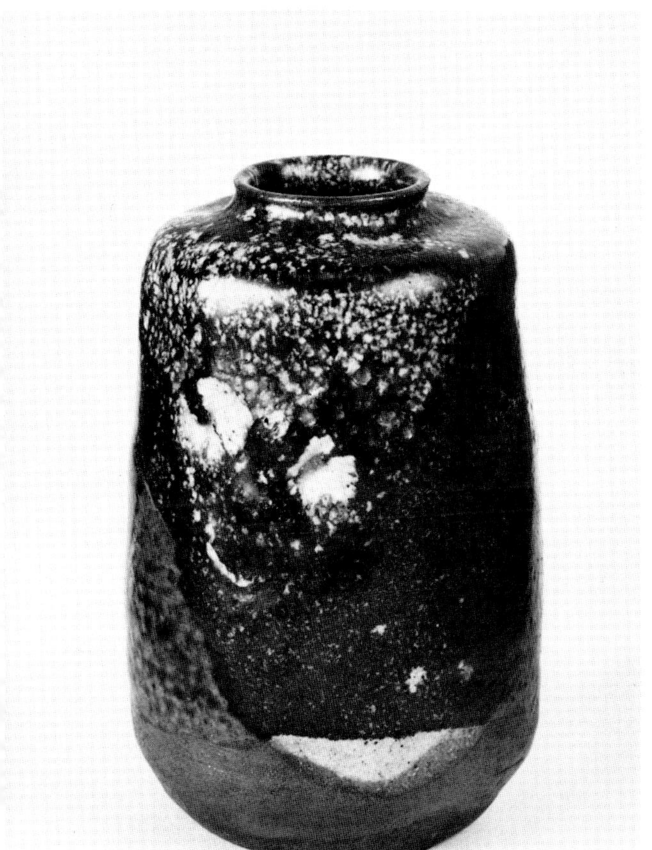

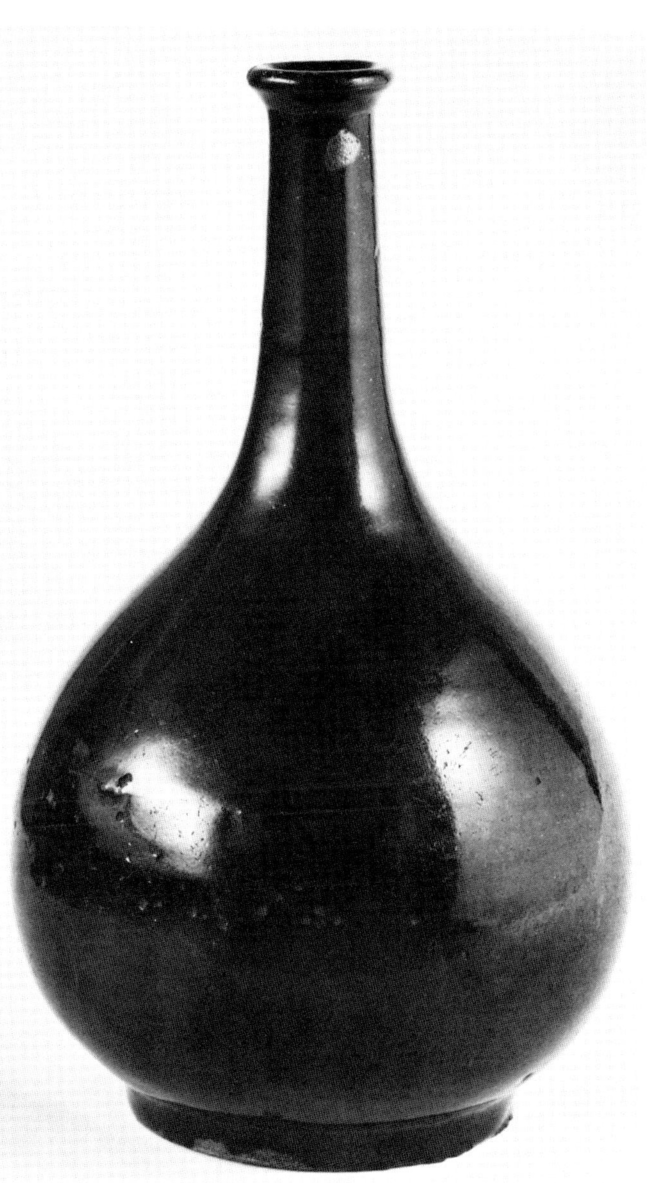

22

Yatsushiro Ware *Mizusashi* (Tea Ceremony Fresh Water Jar)
Edo Period, 17th century.
H: 14.3 cm. (5⅝ in.).
Gray stoneware with stamped designs inlaid with white slip under a semitransparent glaze.
Source and acquisition date unknown X639.6

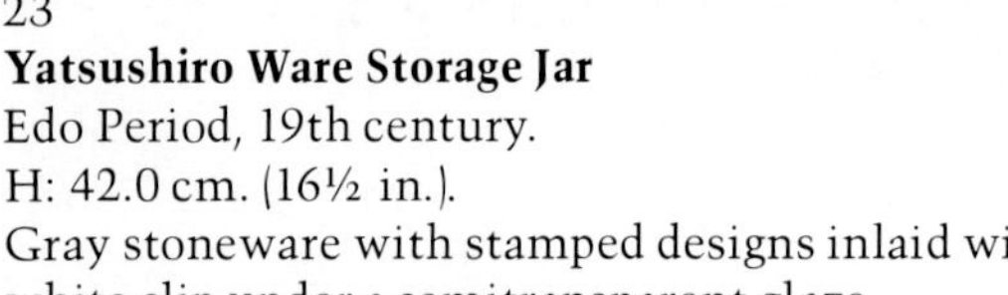

23

Yatsushiro Ware Storage Jar
Edo Period, 19th century.
H: 42.0 cm. (16½ in.).
Gray stoneware with stamped designs inlaid with white slip under a semitransparent glaze.
Gift of Carll H. De Silver 02.32

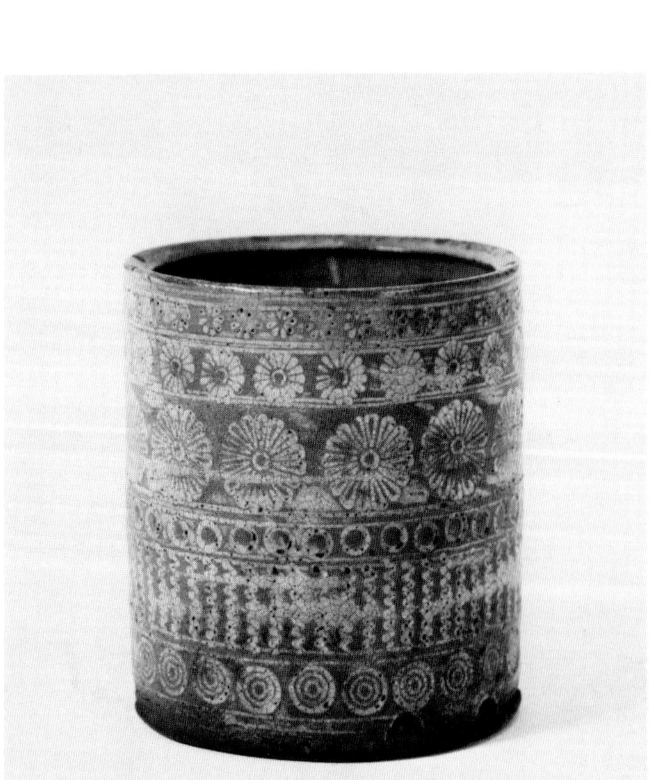

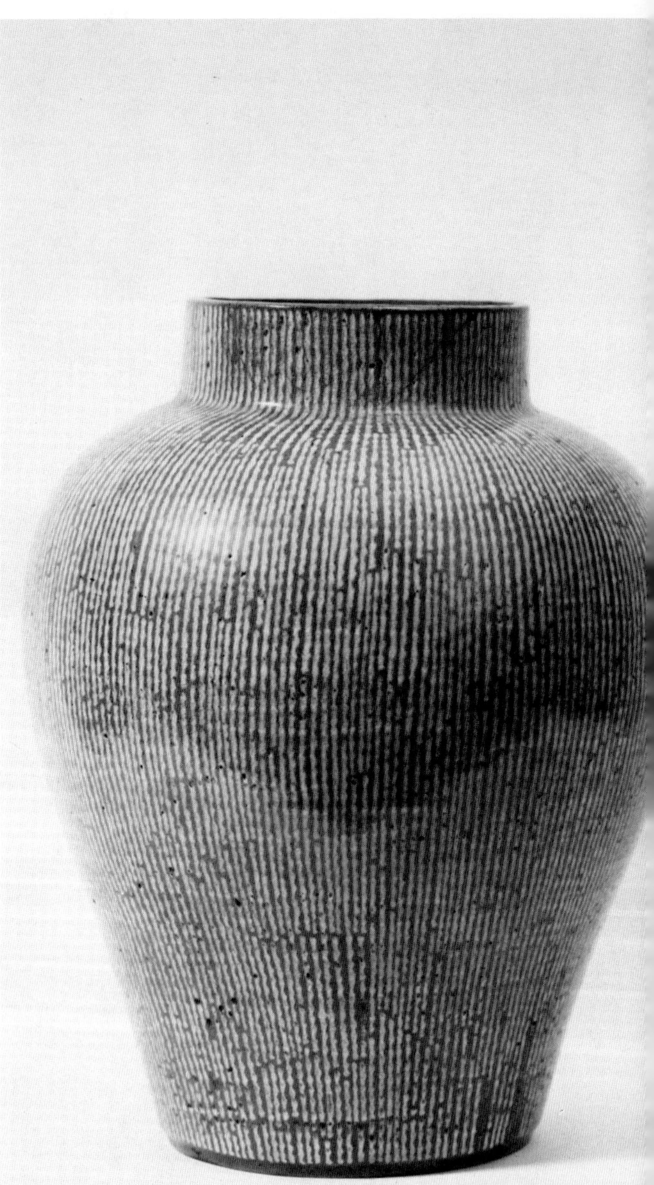

24
E-Shino Ware *Mukōzuke* (Side Dish for the Tea Ceremony Meal)
Momoyama Period, late 16th–early 17th century.
W: 13.3 cm. (5¼ in.).
Buff-white stoneware with iron-brown painted designs under a translucent white glaze.
Lent by Mr. and Mrs. Joseph P. Carroll L78.36.6

25
E-Shino Ware Dish
Edo Period, early 17th century.
W: 22.7 cm. (8 15/16 in.).
Buff-white stoneware with iron-brown painted designs under a transparent white glaze.
Gift of the Mary Livingston Griggs and Mary Griggs Burke Foundation 70.99.1

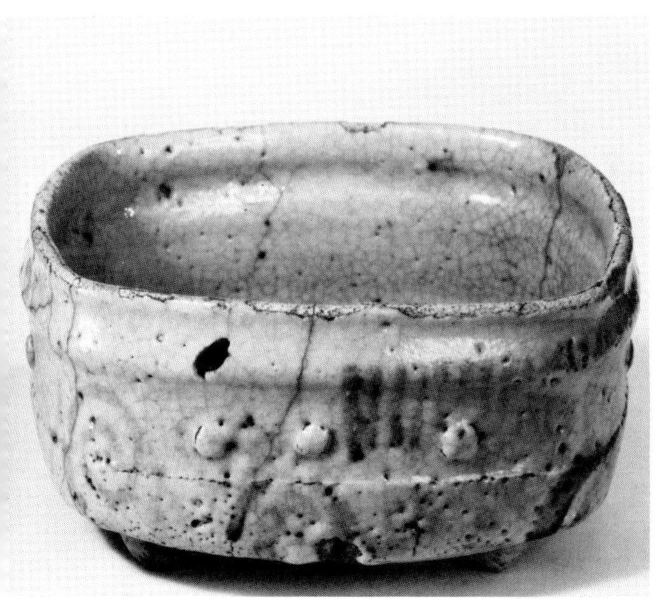

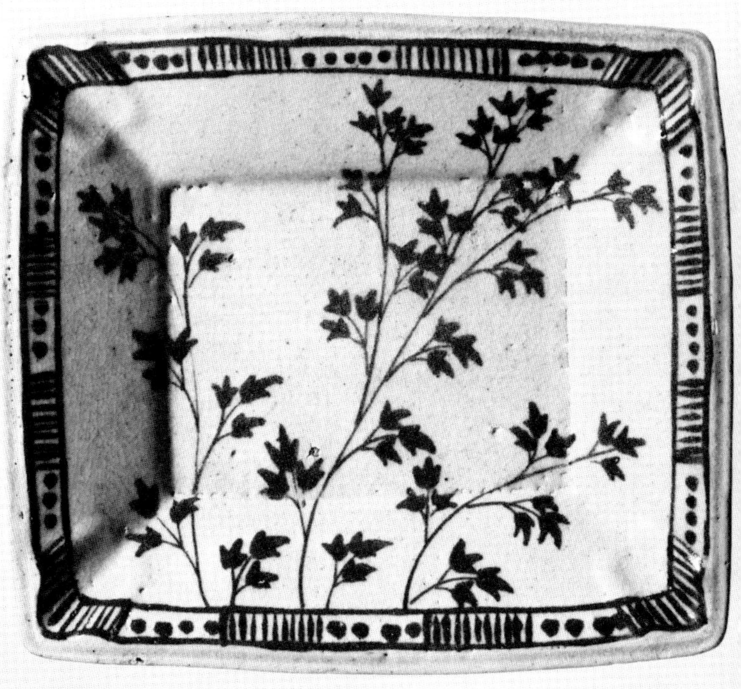

26
Oribe Ware *Mukōzuke* (Side Dish for the Tea Ceremony Meal)
Momoyama Period, early 17th century.
H: 9.5 cm. (3¾ in.).
Buff stoneware; top dipped in green glaze; iron-brown and white-slip painted designs under a clear glaze.
Gift of Robert B. Woodward 03.87

27
Oribe Ware *Mukōzuke* (Side Dish for the Tea Ceremony Meal)
Momoyama Period, early 17th century.
Diam: 15.8 cm. (6¼ in.).
Buff stoneware; edges dipped in green glaze; iron-brown painted designs under a transparent glaze.
Two views are shown below.
Lent by Mr. and Mrs. Joseph P. Carroll L78.67.11

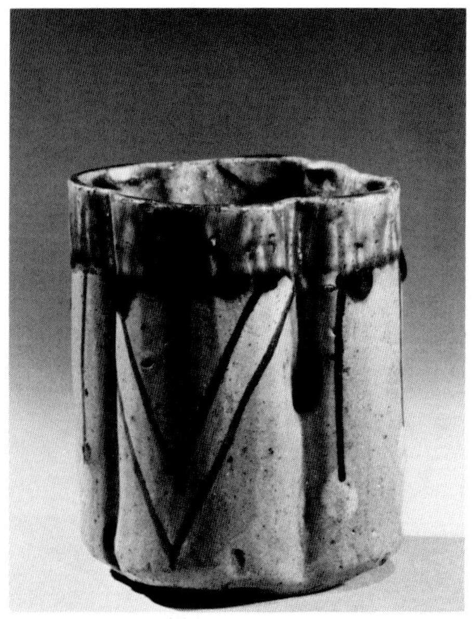

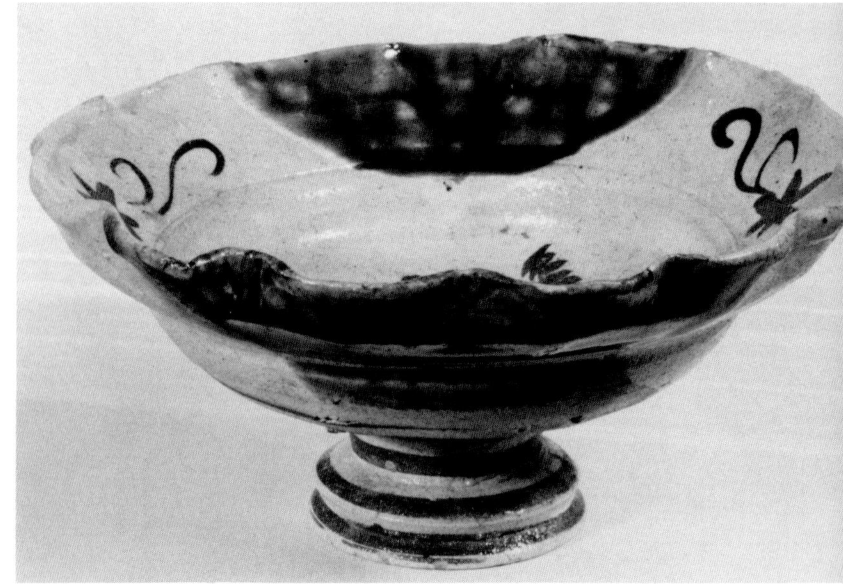

28

Ko-Imari Ware Wine Bottle

Edo Period, late 17th century.
H: 23.5 cm. (9¾ in.).
Blue-and-white porcelain with pomegranate design.
The double-knop neck shape comes from Dutch apothecary bottles.
Gift of Sir George Sansom 74.8.2

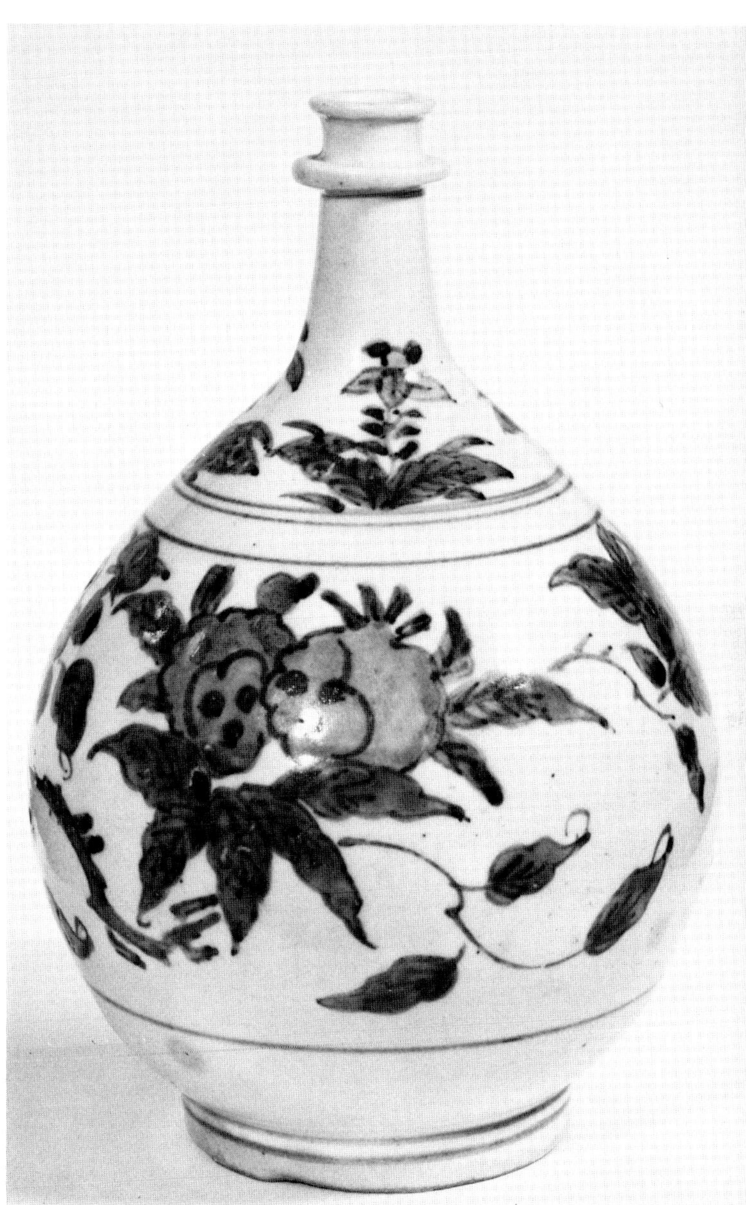

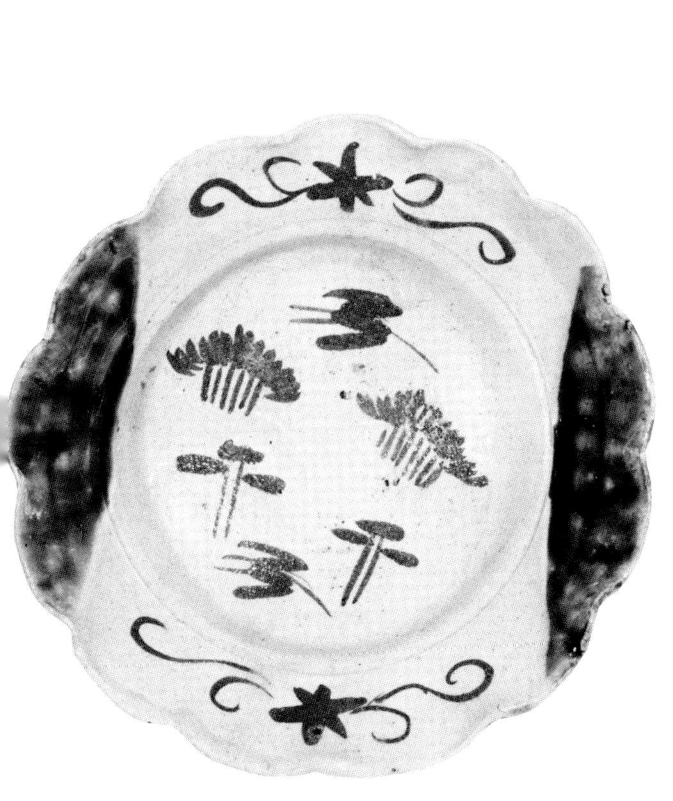

29

Ko-Imari Ware Wine Bottle

Edo Period, late 17th century.
H: 23.5 cm. (9¼ in.).
Blue-and-white porcelain with a design of phoenix and paulownia tree (obverse) and flowering grasses (reverse).
Carll H. De Silver Fund 60.13

30

Ko-Imari Ware Dish

Edo Period, late 17th century.
Diam: 17.8 cm. (7 in.).
Blue-and-white porcelain with bamboo design; *fukizumi* ("blown ink") spattered cobalt blue background.
Gift of Mr. and Mrs. Robert Poster 78.260.1

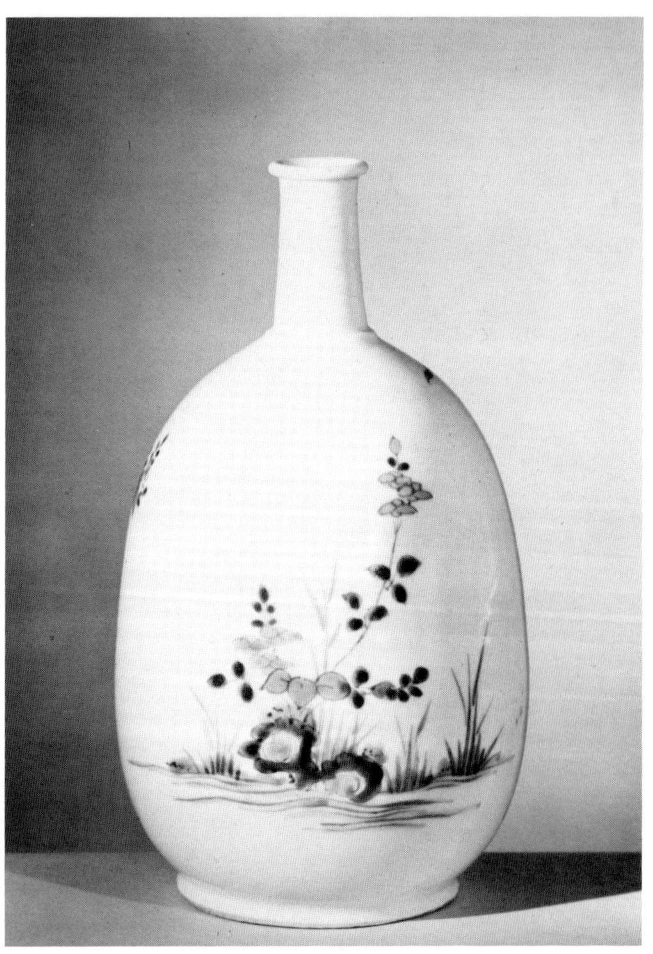

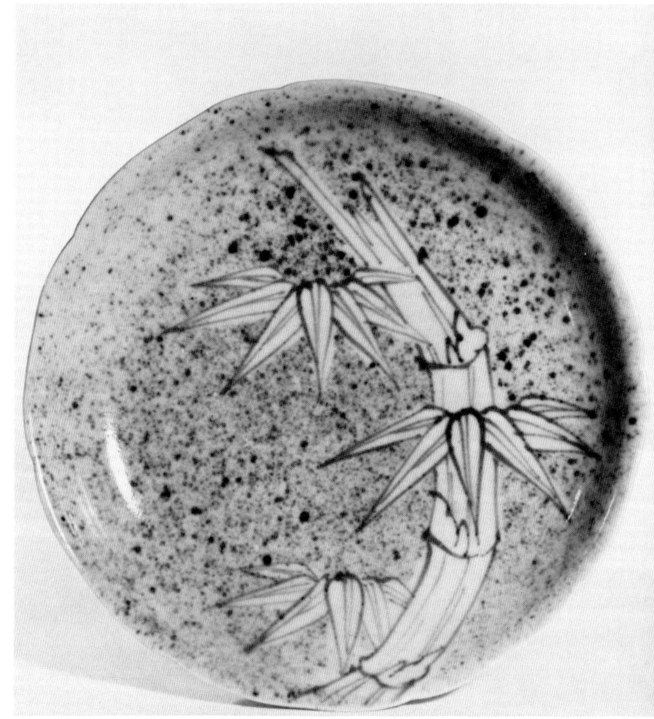

31
Ko-Imari Ware Jar with Cover
Edo Period, late 17th–early 18th century.
H: 68.5 cm. (27 in.).
White porcelain with underglaze blue and overglaze red enamel and gold decoration of grape trellises, landscapes, and chrysanthemums.
Gift of Vernon and Paul Jackne 30.1099

32
Ko-Imari Ware Octagonal Plate
Edo Period, late 17th–early 18th century.
Diam: 28.5 cm. (11¼ in.).
White porcelain with openwork rondels; underglaze blue and overglaze red enamel and gold decoration of birds and flowers.
Gift of the Executors of the Estate of Augustus Hutchins 74.55.4

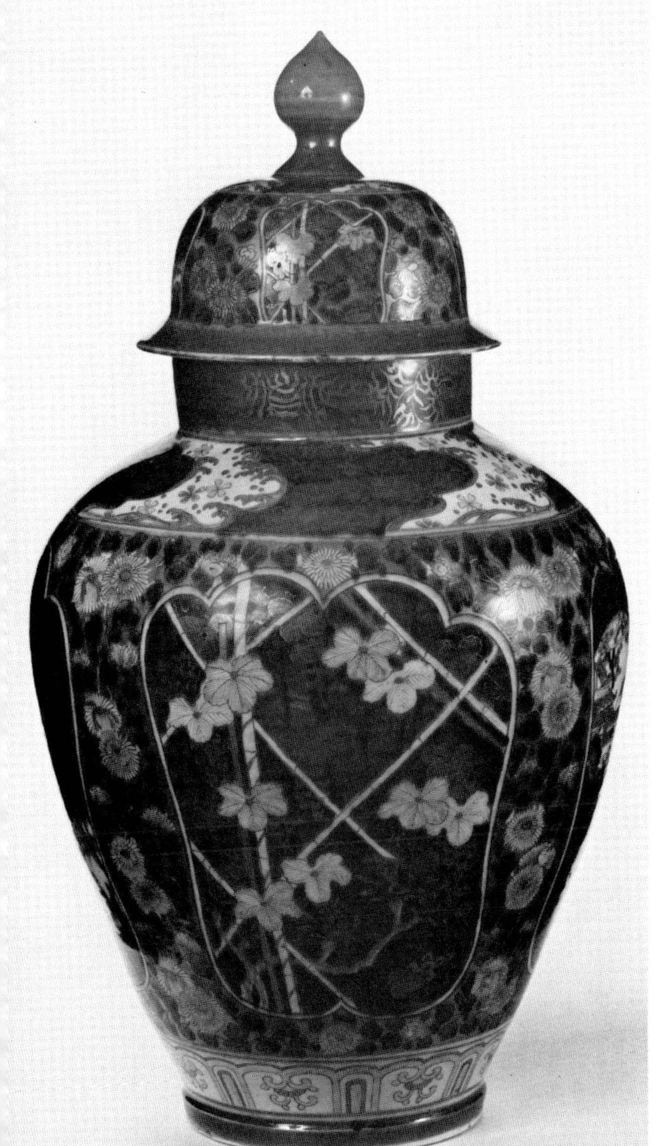

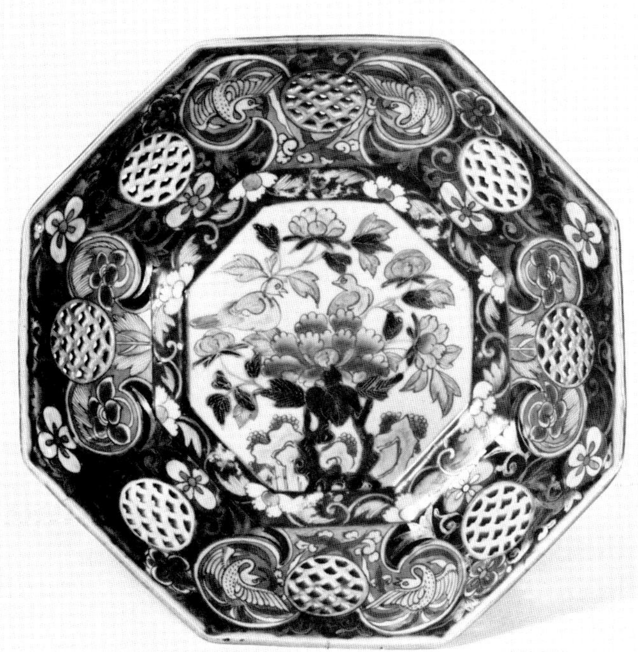

33
Imari Ware Bowl
Edo Period, early 19th century.
Diam: 11.2 cm. (4⅜ in.).
White porcelain with underglaze blue and overglaze red, black, and green enamel and gold decoration of Dutchmen and a Dutch ship.
Gift of the Executors of the Estate of Augustus Hutchins 52.87.2

34
Kakiemon Ware Bowl
Edo Period, late 17th century.
Diam: 14.7 cm. (5¾ in.).
White porcelain with red, green, yellow, blue, and black overglaze enamel decoration.
Gift of Dr. and Mrs. Frank L. Babbott 74.55.3

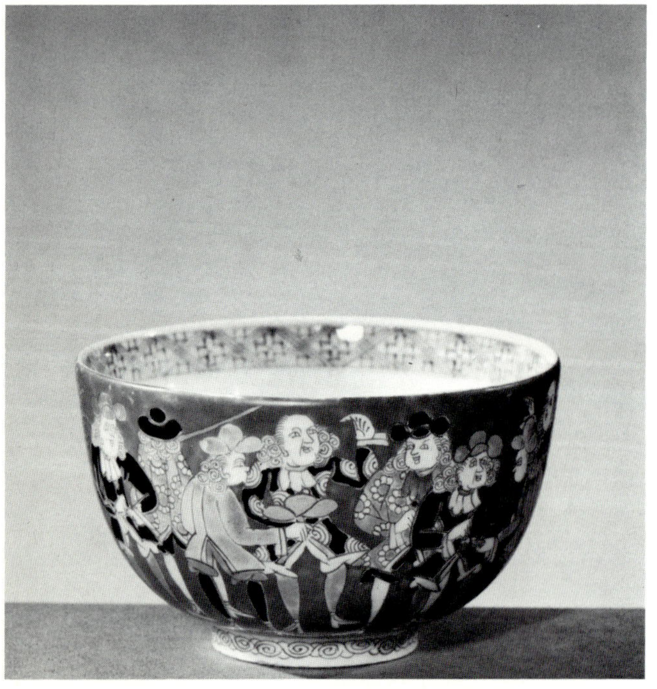

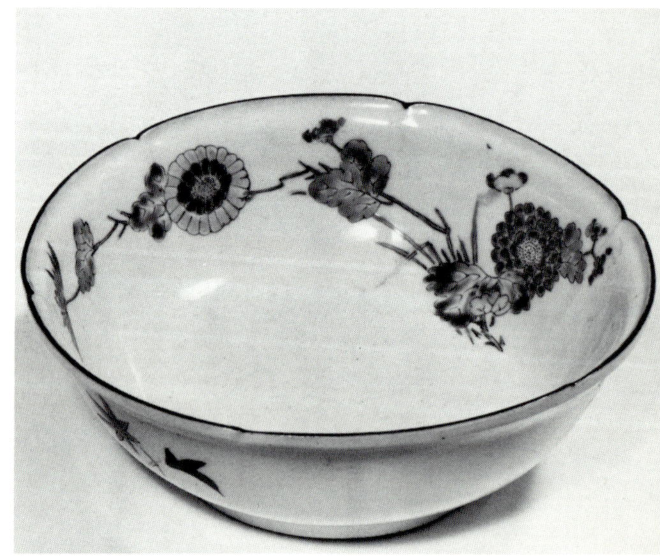

35
Kakiemon Ware Dish
Edo Period, 18th century.
Diam: 19 cm. (7½ in.).
White porcelain with red, blue, green, and yellow overglaze enamel and gold decoration.
Museum Purchase 75.127.1

36
Nabeshima Ware Dish
Edo Period, 18th century.
Diam: 20.6 cm. (8⅛ in.).
White porcelain with underglaze blue and overglaze red and yellow enamel decoration; celadon glaze on lip.
Museum Purchase 60.202

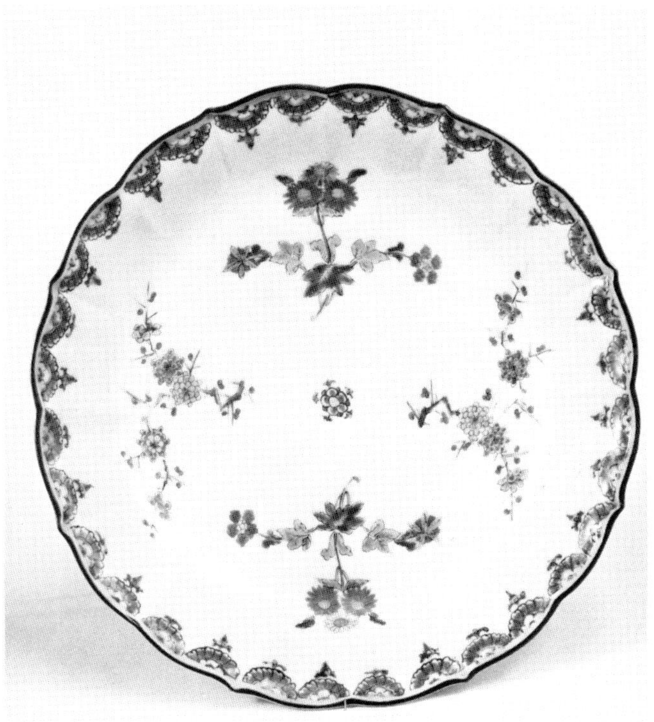

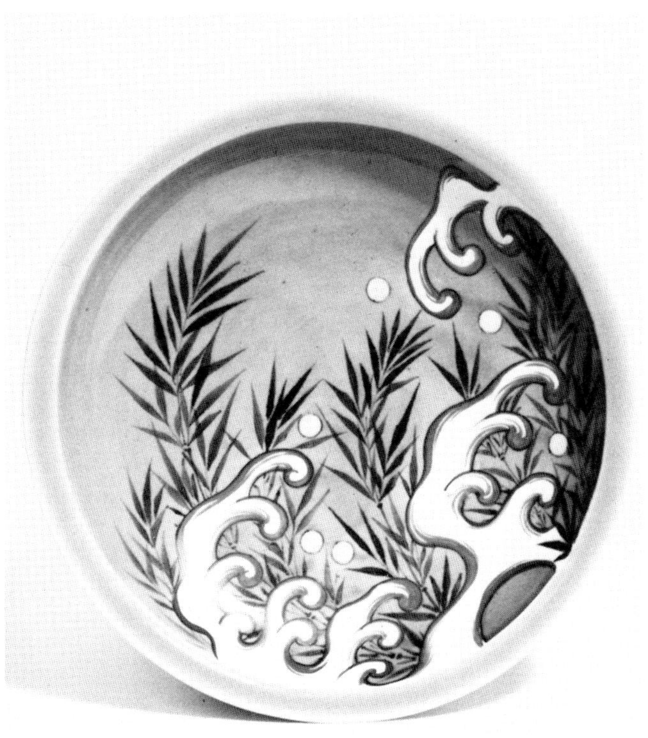

37 *Illustrated in color on the front cover.*
Ko-Kutani Ware Dish
Edo Period, second half of the 17th century.
L: 15.8 cm. (6¼ in.).
White porcelain with underglaze blue and overglaze red, purple, green, blue, and black enamel decoration.
Lent by Dr. John Lyden L79.9.1

38
Ko-Kutani Ware Plate
Edo Period, second half of the 17th century.
Diam: 23.8 cm. (9⅜ in.).
White porcelain with green, yellow, purple, blue, red, and black overglaze enamel decoration.
Gift of Mr. and Mrs. Samuel H. Lindenbaum 75.174

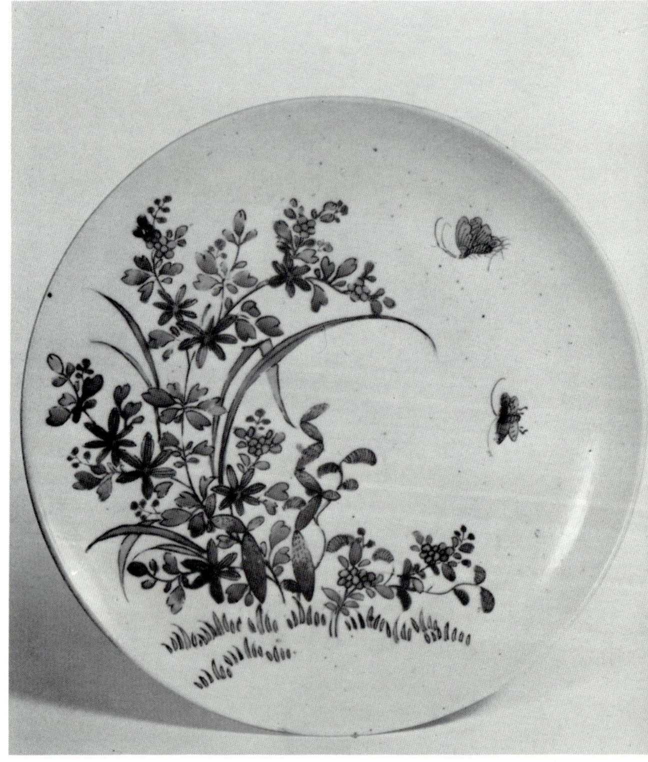

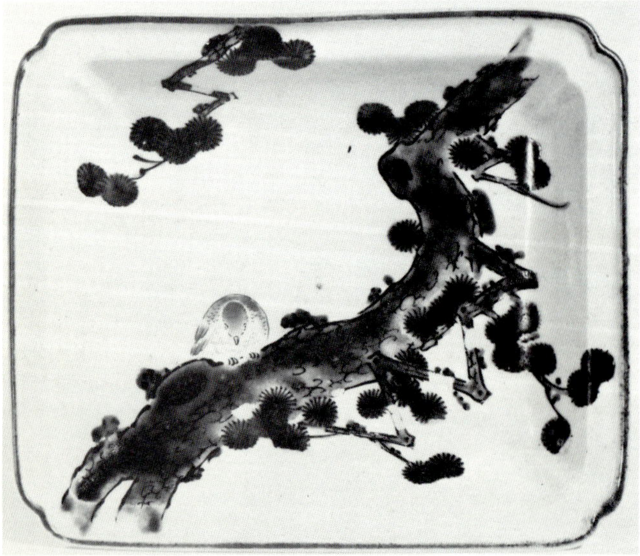

39
Kutani Ware Bowl
Edo Period, early 19th century.
Yoshidaya Kiln
Diam: 24.8 cm. (9¾ in.).
White porcelain with green, yellow, purple, blue, and black overglaze enamel decoration.
Anonymous Gift 75.201

40
Incense Burner in the Form of a Pheasant
Edo Period, 17th century.
Attributed to **Nonomura Ninsei** died *circa* 1660
L: 44.5 cm. (17½ in.).
Tan earthenware with overglaze brown, black, blue, and red enamel and gold decoration.
Gift of Howard Hollis 78.253

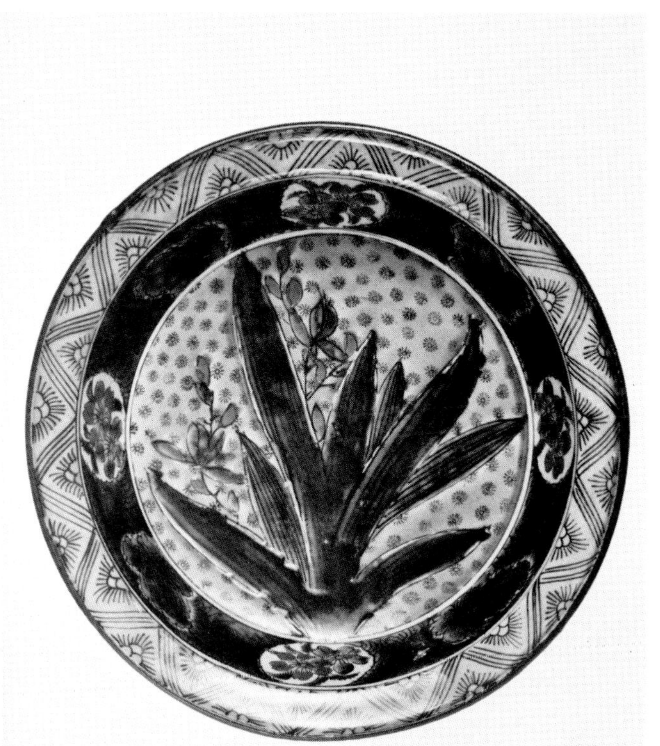

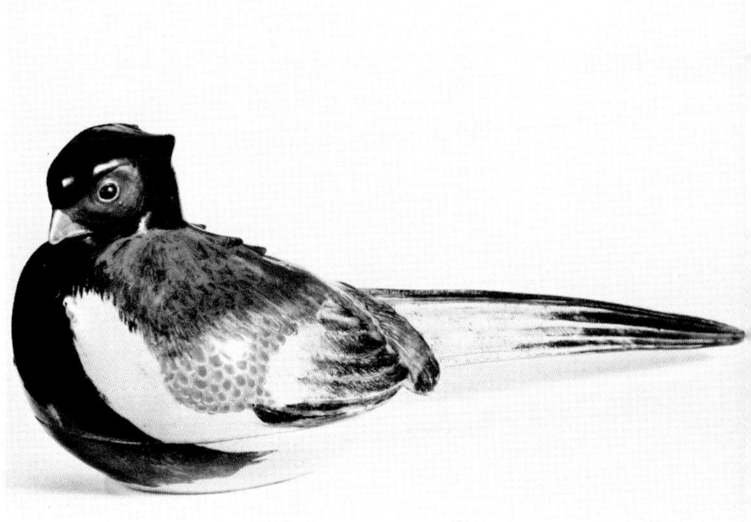

41
Ko-Kiyomizu Ware *Chōshi* (Rice Wine Ewer)
Edo Period, 18th century.
H: 8.8 cm. (3½ in.).
Tan earthenware with overglaze blue, green, and red enamel and gold decoration.
Lent by Charles Brandon L78.35

42
Ko-Kiyomizu Ware Incense Burner in the Form of a Cloth Bag
Edo Period, 18th century.
H: 10.2 cm. (4 in.).
Tan earthenware with overglaze green and blue enamel and gold decoration.
Lent by Dr. John Lyden L78.71.2

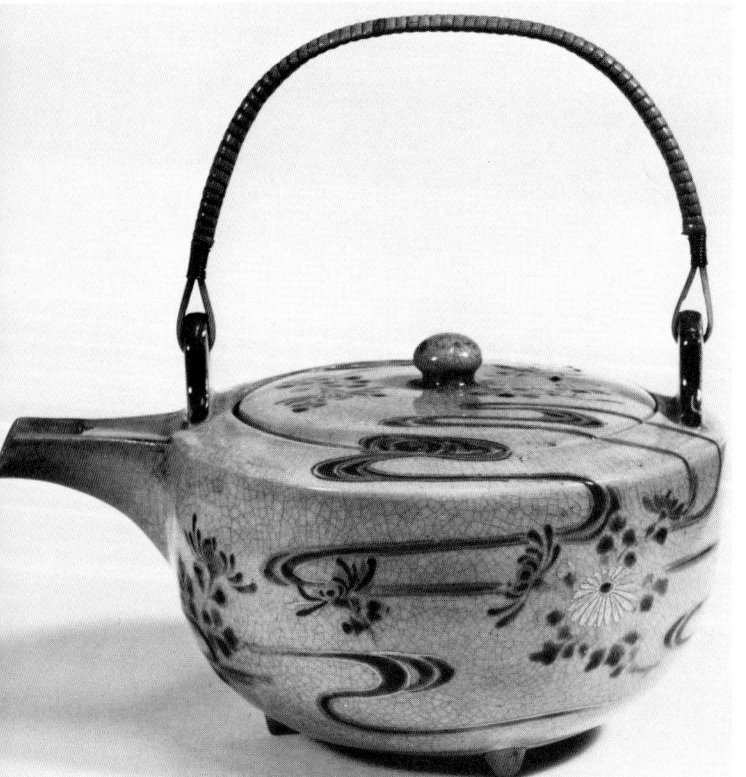

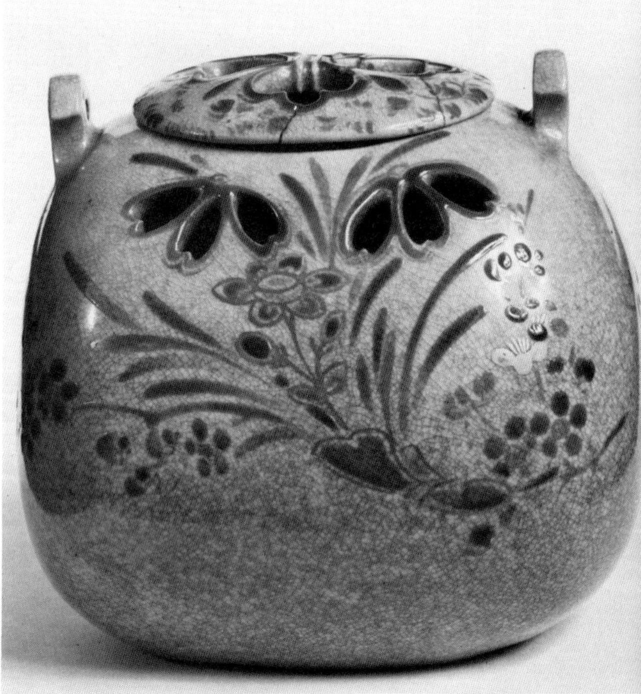

3
Ko-Kiyomizu Ware Incense Burner in the Form of a lower-Arranging Basket
do Period, 18th century.
H: 15.9 cm. (6¼ in.).
'an earthenware with overglaze green and blue namel and gold decoration.
ent by Mr. and Mrs. Joseph P. Carroll L78.67.12

44
Square Dish with the God of Longevity Reading a Scroll
Edo Period, 17th–18th century.
Dish, decoration, and inscription **Ogata Kenzan** 1663–1743.
Figure of Jurōjin and its signature **Ogata Kōrin** 1658–1716.
H: 2.7 cm. (1⅛ in.), W: 21.8 cm. (8⅝ in.).
Tan earthenware with underglaze iron-oxide brown-black painted decoration.
Published: Soame Jenyns, *Japanese Pottery* (London, 1971), pl. 98B.
A.A. Healy Fund 40.505

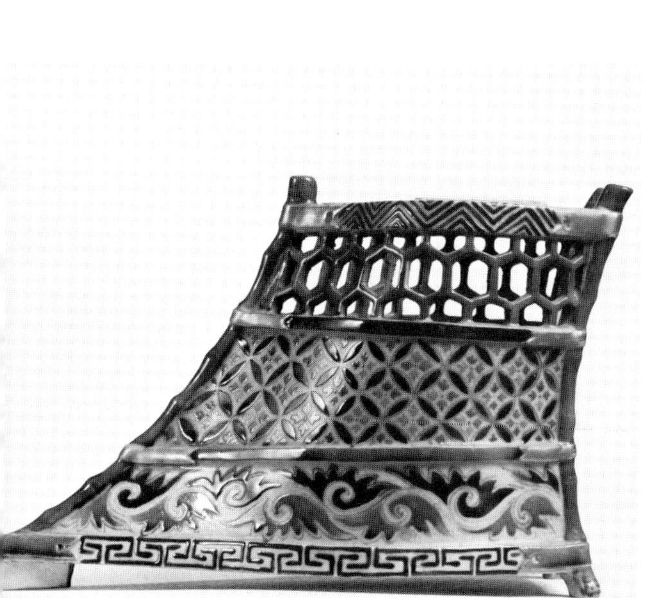

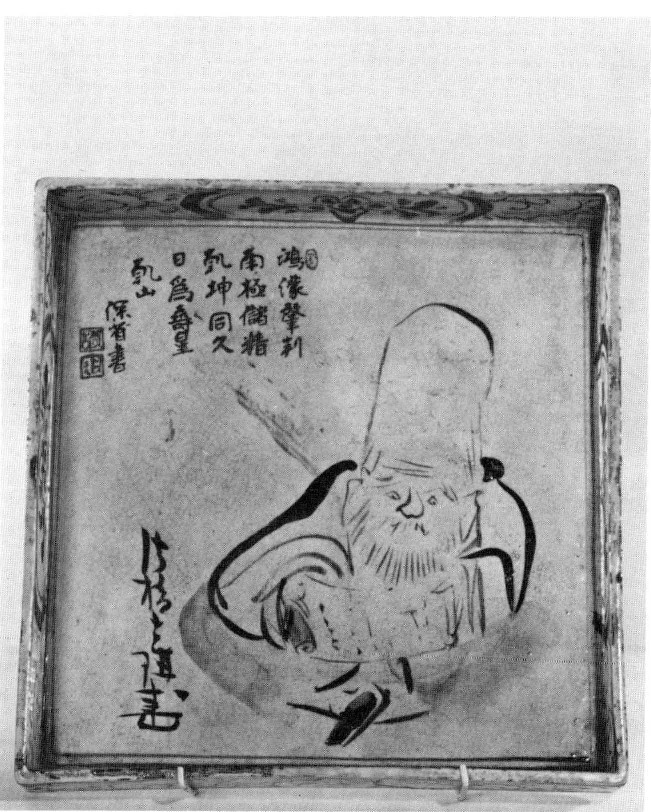

45 *Illustrated in color on the back cover.*
Mukōzuke **(Side Dish for the Tea Ceremony Meal) with Camellia Design**
Edo Period, 18th century.
Ogata Kenzan 1663–1743
H: 5.5 cm. ($2\frac{3}{16}$ in.).
Tan earthenware with overglaze green enamel background; wax-resist blossoms with yellow enamel centers. Underglaze iron-oxide brown-black signature, "Kenzan," on base is illustrated below right.
Gift of the J. Aron Charitable Foundation 78.208

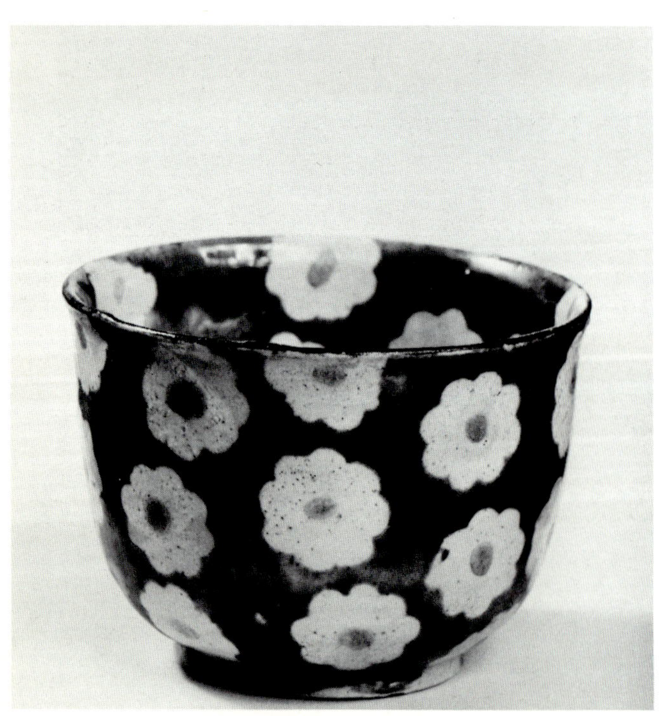

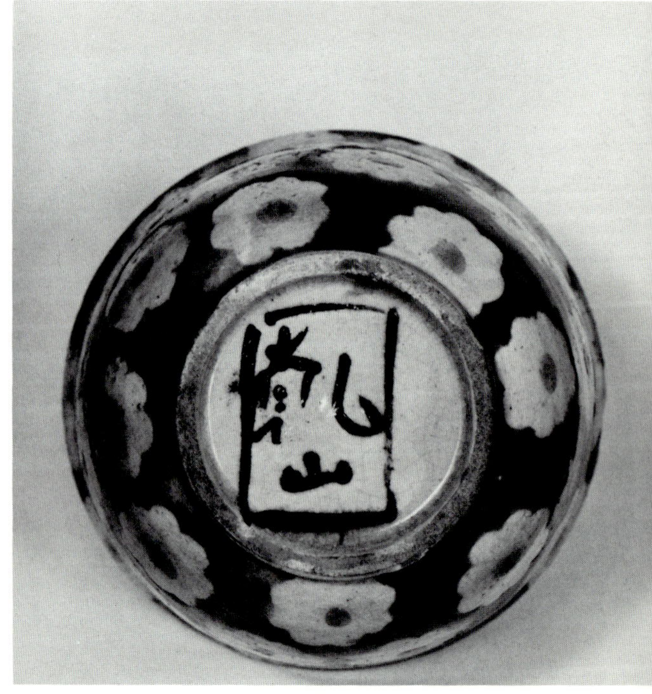

46
Mino-Kasahara Ware Large Bowl
Edo Period, 17th century.
H: 10.2 cm. (4 in.), Diam: 35.6 cm. (14 in.).
Gray stoneware with greenish tan glaze; underglaze iron-oxide brown-black painted decoration of reeds.
Museum Purchase 74.109.1

47
Futagawa Ware Large Bowl
Edo Period, 18th century.
H: 16.2 cm. (6⅜ in.), Diam: 50.2 cm. (19⅞ in.).
Gray stoneware with reddish brown surface where exposed; *hakeme* (brushed-on white slip) ground with pine branch and moon painted in brown and green under a clear glaze; finger-combed wave pattern through white slip on upper half of exterior.
Gift of the Tokyo Marine and Fire Insurance Co. 75.124

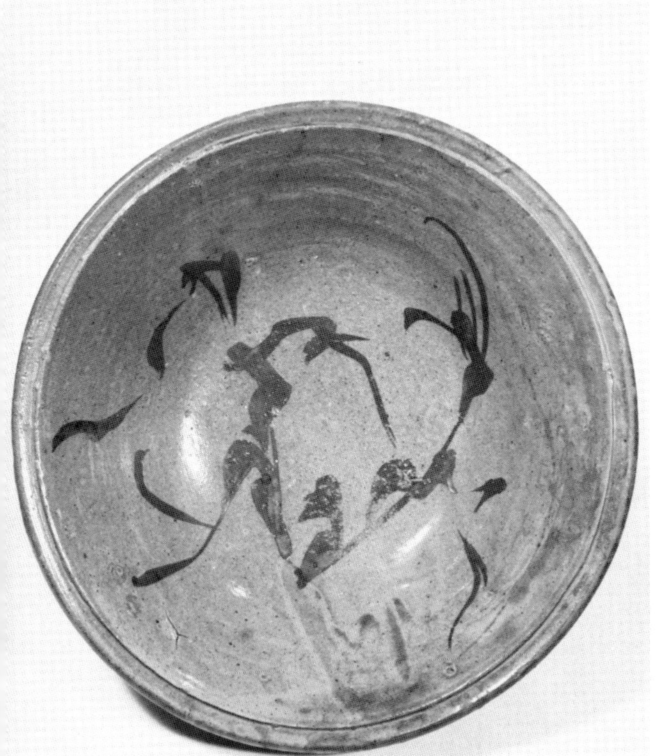

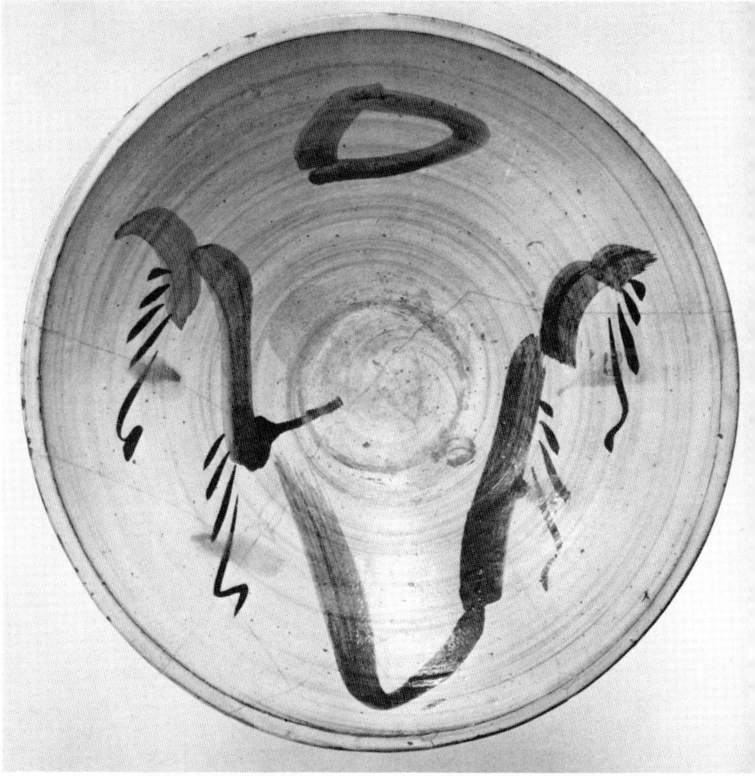

48

Seto Ware Oil Plate

Edo Period, early 19th century.
Diam: 22.3 cm. (8¾ in.).
Tan stoneware with a cream-colored glaze; underglaze iron-oxide brown-black painted design of a kiosk near trees by the shore of a lake with a flight of wild geese above.
Gift of Willard Straight 38.146

49

Seto Ware Herring Plate

Edo Period, early 19th century.
Diam: 36.2 cm. (14¼ in.).
Tan stoneware with a clear glaze over iron-brown and cobalt blue painted decoration of flowers by a stream.
Gift of Dr. Bertram Schaffner 74.108.2

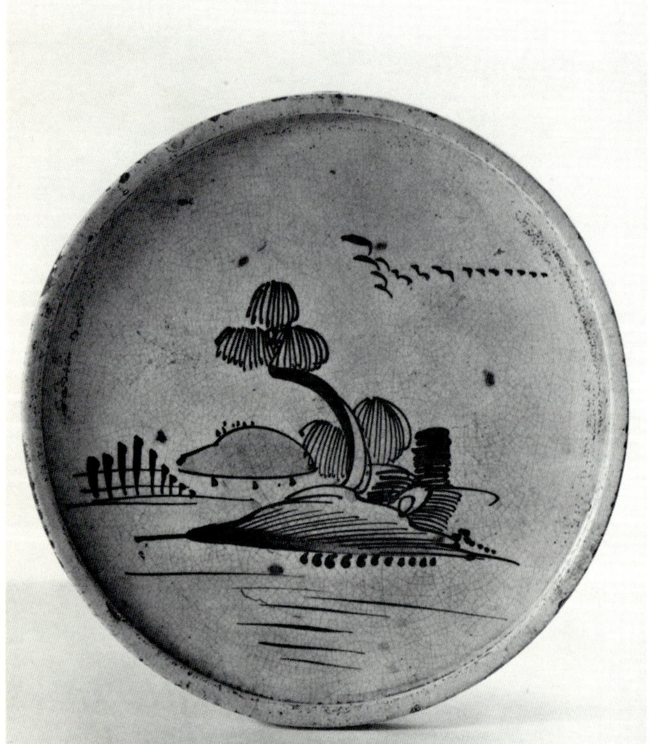

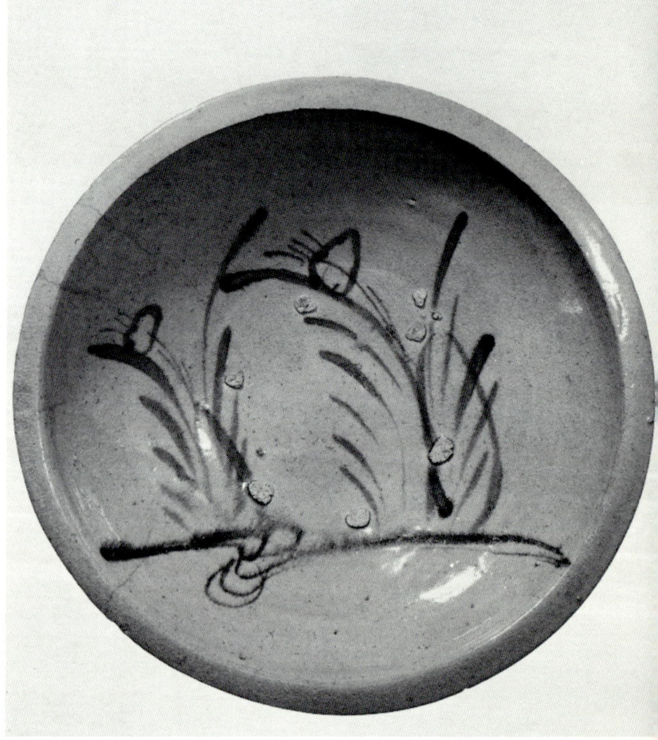

50
Seto Ware Horse-Eye Plate
Edo Period, early 19th century.
Diam: 25.8 cm. (10 3/16 in.).
Tan stoneware with cream-colored glaze over iron-oxide brown-black painted designs of concentric circles.
Gift of Willard Straight 38.149

51
Shigaraki Ware Wine Bottle
Edo Period, first half of the 19th century.
H: 26.0 cm. (10¼ in.).
Tan stoneware with a thick green glaze on the neck and shoulder running in finger-like drips into the clear glaze on the remainder of the vessel.
Lent by Mr. and Mrs. Joseph P. Carroll L78.67.14

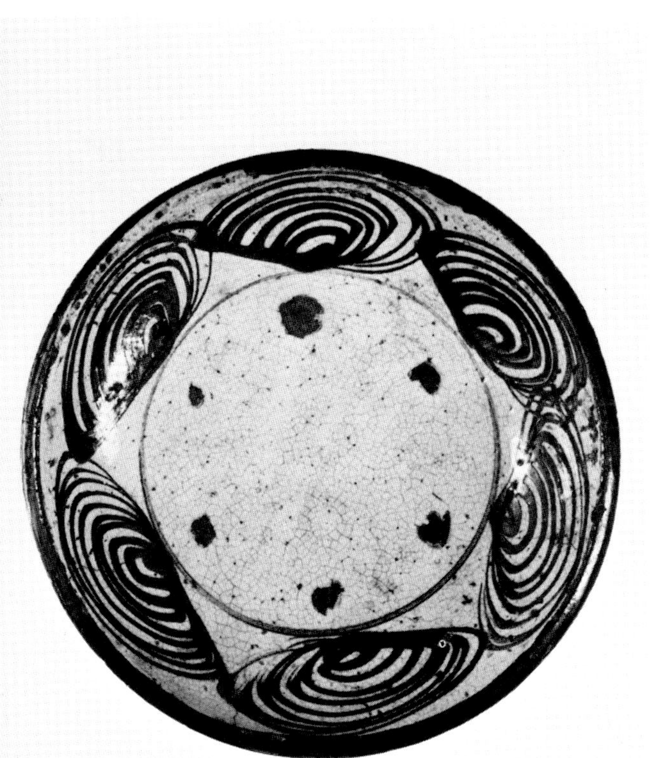

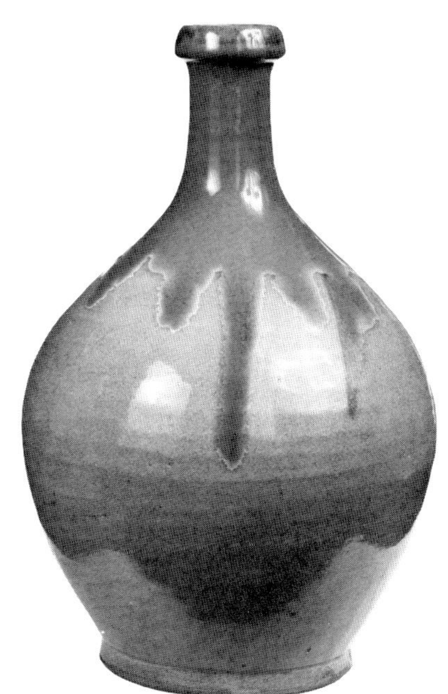

52
Shigaraki Ware Water Jar
Edo Period, first half of the 19th century.
H: 52.1 cm. (20½ in.).
Buff stoneware with a cream-white glaze decorated with long pours of alternating blue and green glaze.
Lent by Margery and Harry Kahn L76.49.2

53
Tamba Ware Wine Bottle
Edo Period, first half of the 19th century.
H: 26.7 cm. (10½ in.).
Gray stoneware with decoration of white-slip rings and zigzags trailed from a bamboo tube covered with a clear glaze.
Lent by Mr. and Mrs. Joseph P. Carroll L78.67.13

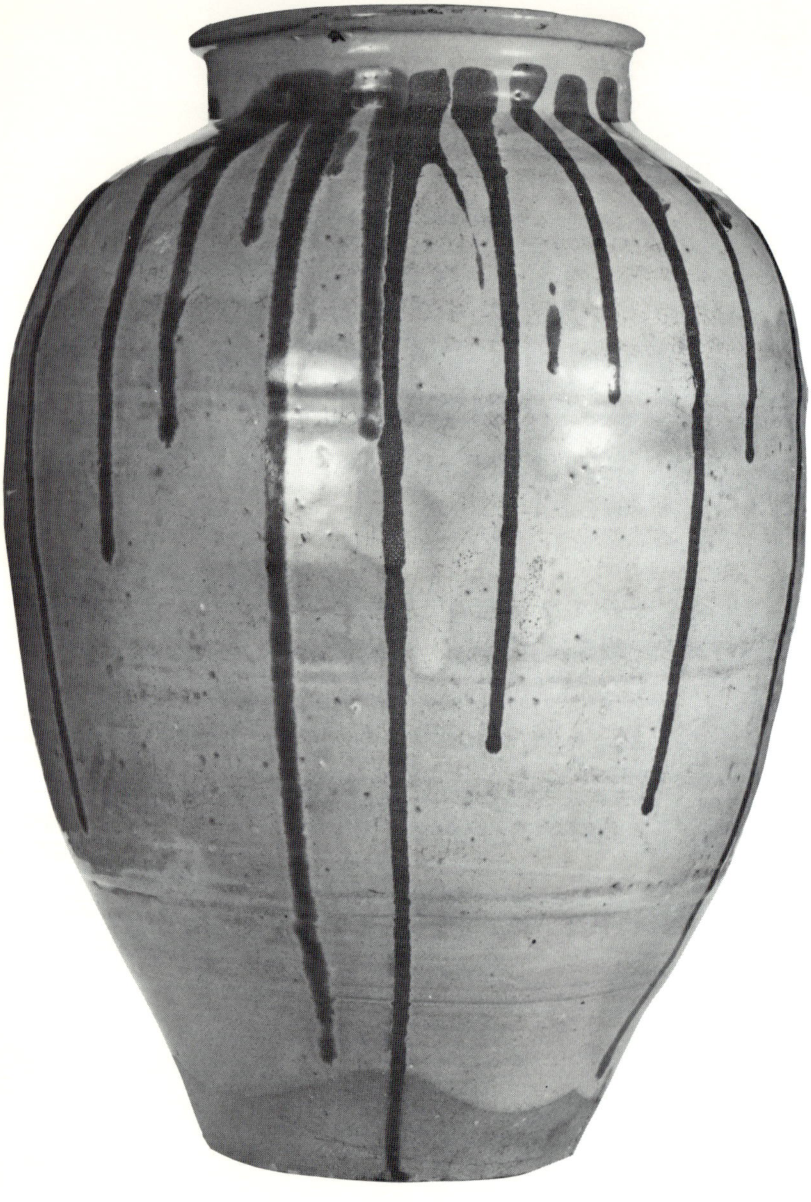

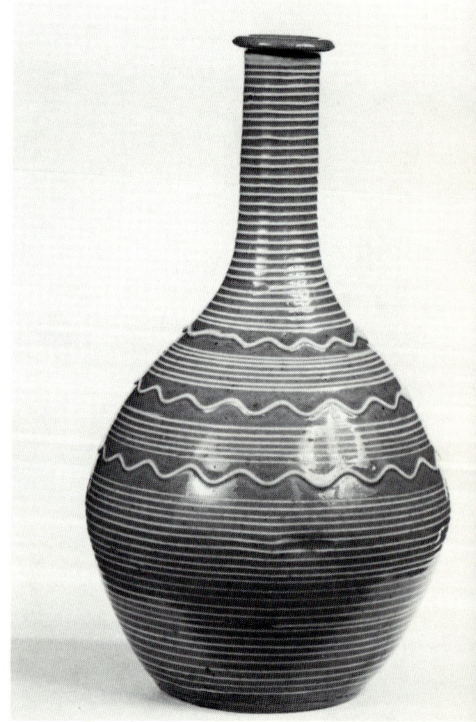

54

Blue-and-White Porcelain Green-Tea Set

Meiji Period, late 19th–early 20th century.
Seifū Yohei III 1851–1914.
Cups: H: 5.1 cm. (2 in.), Diam: 8.2 cm. (3¼ in.).
Underglaze cobalt painted decoration of grass orchids (epidendrons).
Gift of Jeanette Rothbard 76.186.1a-h
[This famous porcelain artist worked in Kyoto.]

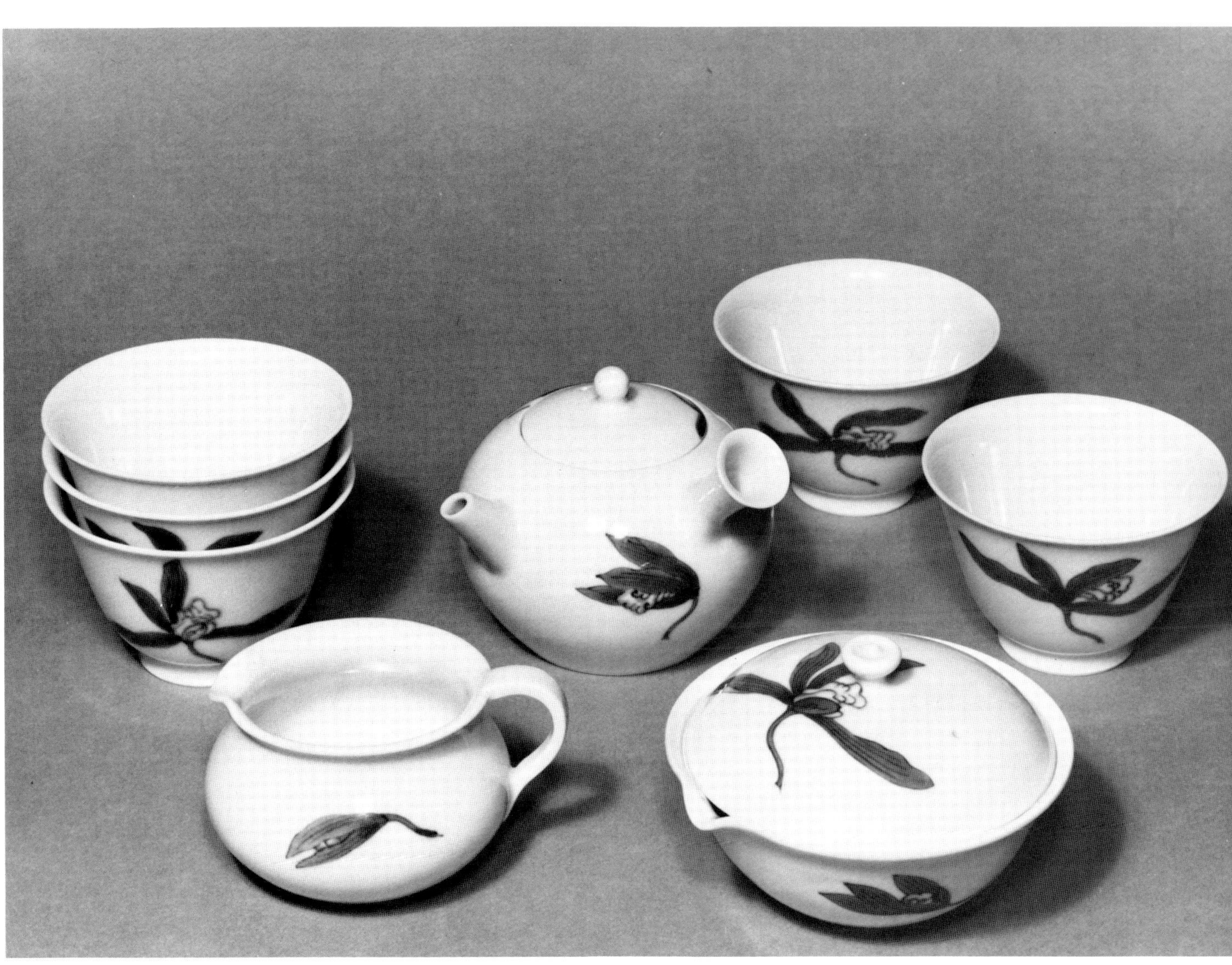

55
Large Stoneware Black-Glazed Bottle-Vase
Shōwa Period, *circa* 1960.
Bernard Leach born 1887.
H: 39.1 cm. (15⅜ in.).
Temmoku iron-oxide glazed bottle made at Hamada's kiln in Mashiko; form thrown round and then pressed flat on four sides.
Lent by Michael Kan L76.4

56
Square Plate
Shōwa Period, *circa* 1960.
Hamada Shōji 1894–1977.
W: 31.7 cm. (12½ in.).
Stoneware with a crawled, sand-colored glaze; wheat stalk motif painted in iron-oxide brown; mottled iron-tan and brown border with stamped hatched pattern.
Gift of Margery and Harry Kahn 75.179

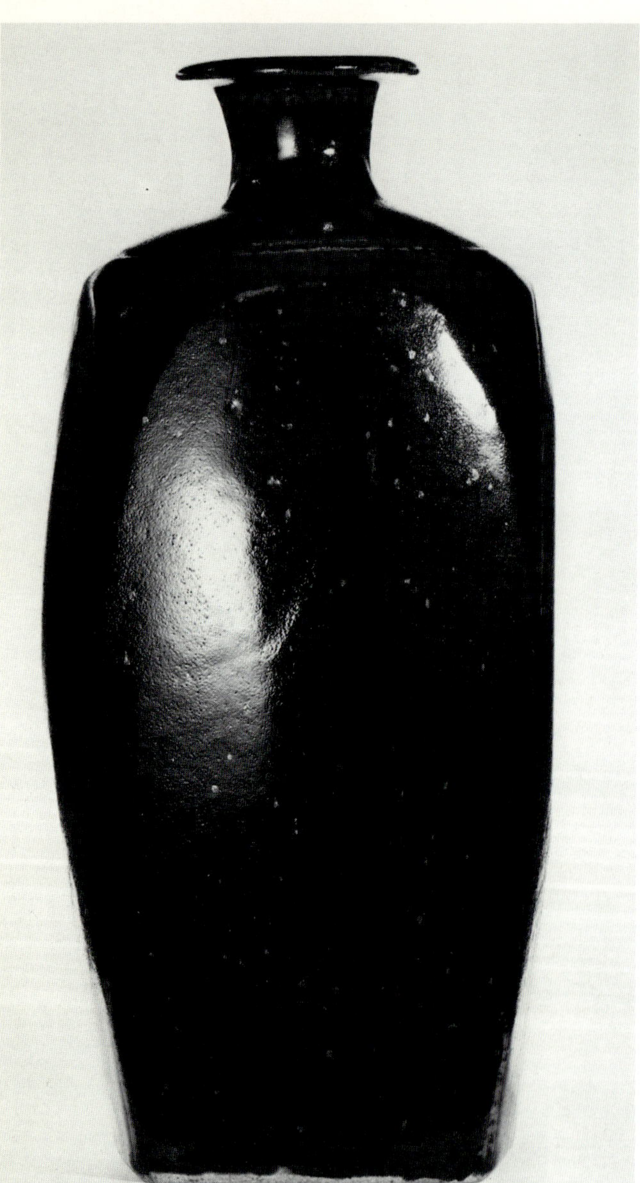

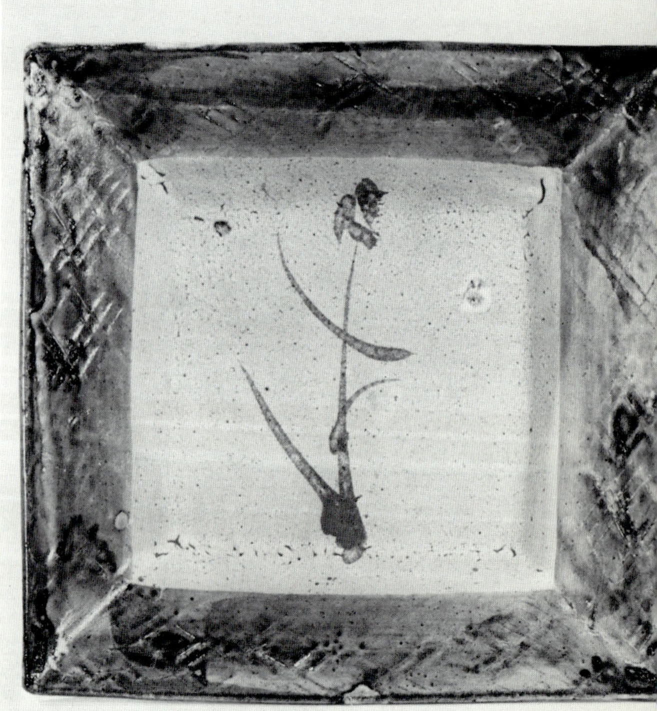

57

Black-Glazed Octagonal Stoneware Bottle-Vase

Shōwa Period, *circa* 1960.

Hamada Shōji 1894–1977.

H: 27.0 cm. (10⅝ in.).

Temmoku iron-oxide glazed bottle; *mentori* (thrown round, then sides cut off flat with a potter's knife).

Gift of Alice Boney 76.66

58

Tea Bowl

Shōwa Period, *circa* 1940.

Kawai Kanjirō 1890–1966.

H: 8.7 cm. (3⅜ in.).

Buff stoneware with a chevron and blossom design in wax-resist on an iron-brown ground under a clear glaze.

Anonymous Gift 40.723

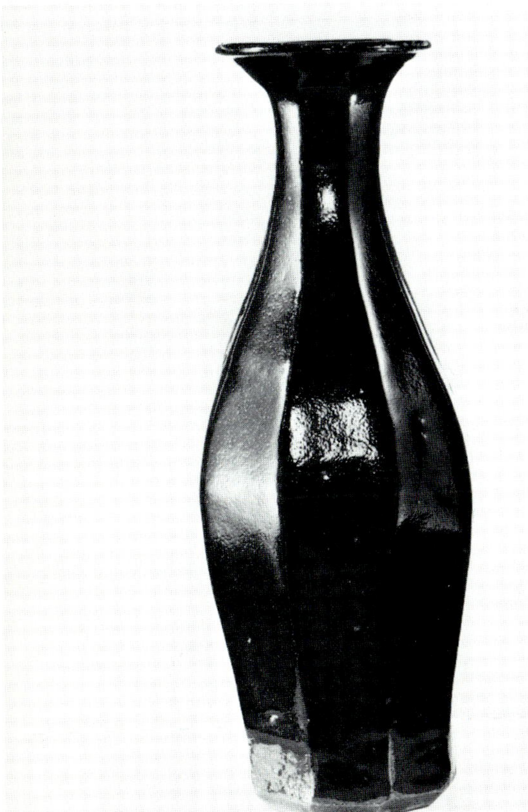

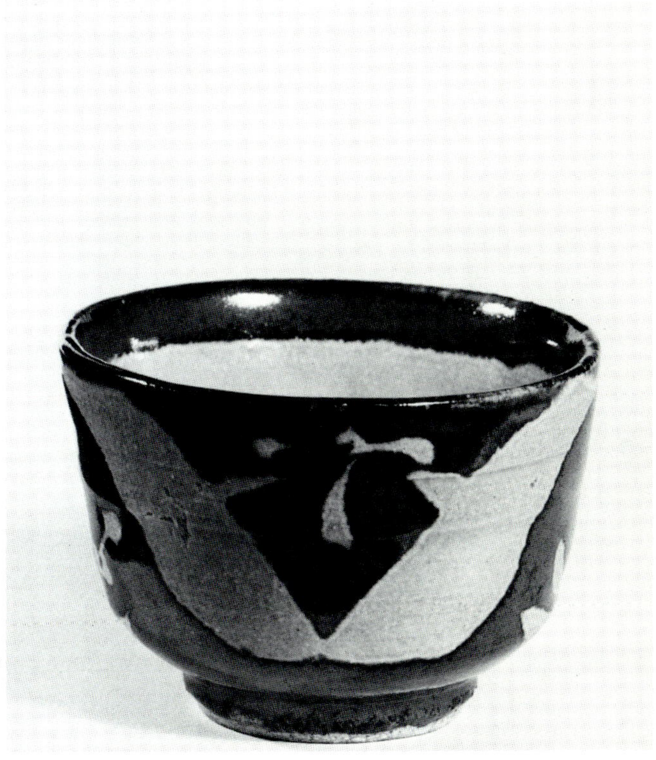

59
Tea Bowl
Shōwa Period, *circa* 1960.
Kawai Kanjirō 1890–1966.
H: 10.2 cm. (4 in.).
Buff stoneware with a clear, slightly bluish glaze; most of exterior covered with underglaze copper red (*shinsha*); trailed-slip floral decoration.
Lent by Sonia Kroyt L76.65

60
Tea Cup
Shōwa Period, *circa* 1950.
Kawai Kanjirō 1890–1966.
H: 7.6 cm. (3 in.).
Buff stoneware with a clear, slightly bluish glaze; most of exterior covered with underglaze *gosu* (mottled, dark blue, unrefined cobalt oxide); trailed-slip floral decoration.
Gift of Dr. Herbert Meadow 75.120.4
[This is a *yunomi*, a small cup made for drinking ordinary steeped green tea. (A *chawan* is the larger bowl used for drinking the whipped powdered green tea in the tea ceremony.)]

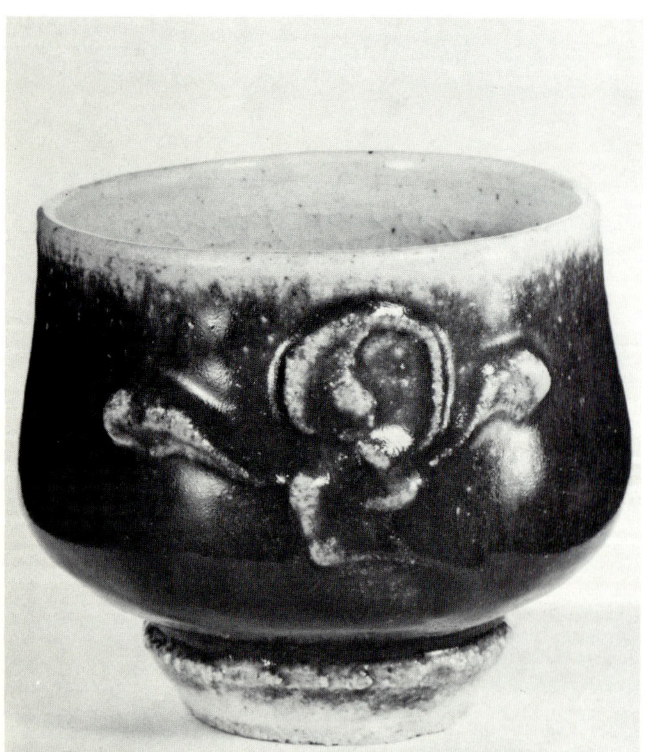

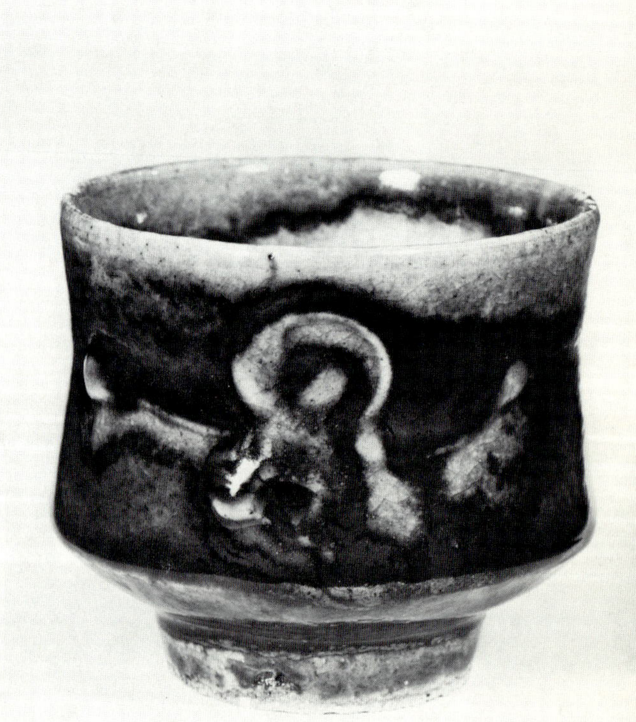

61
Vase
Shōwa Period, *circa* 1955.
Kawai Kanjirō 1890–1966.
H: 18.5 cm. (7¼ in.).
Stoneware vase formed in a slab mold; clear glaze over a ground of unrefined cobalt blue; slip-trailed floral ornament touched with underglaze red, brown, and black.
Gift of Dr. Herbert Meadow 75.120.2

62
Bottle Vase
Shōwa Period, *circa* 1965.
Kawai Kanjirō 1890–1966.
H: 24.7 cm. (9¾ in.).
Slab-mold–built bottle of a coarse stoneware (Shigaraki clay) with splashed abstract decoration of red, brown, green, and light gray under a clear glaze.
Gift of Dr. Herbert Meadow 75.120.1

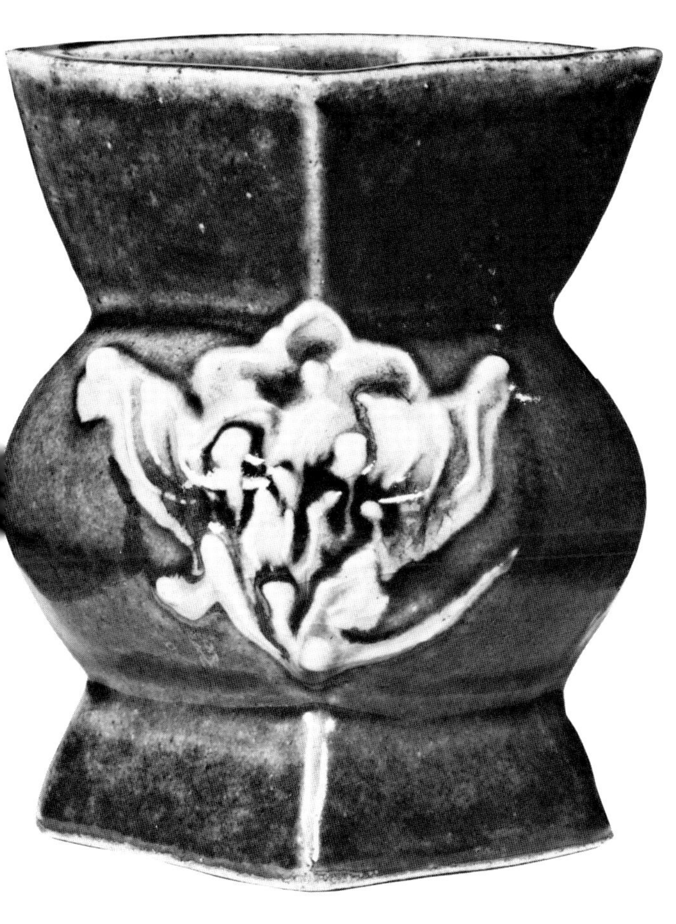

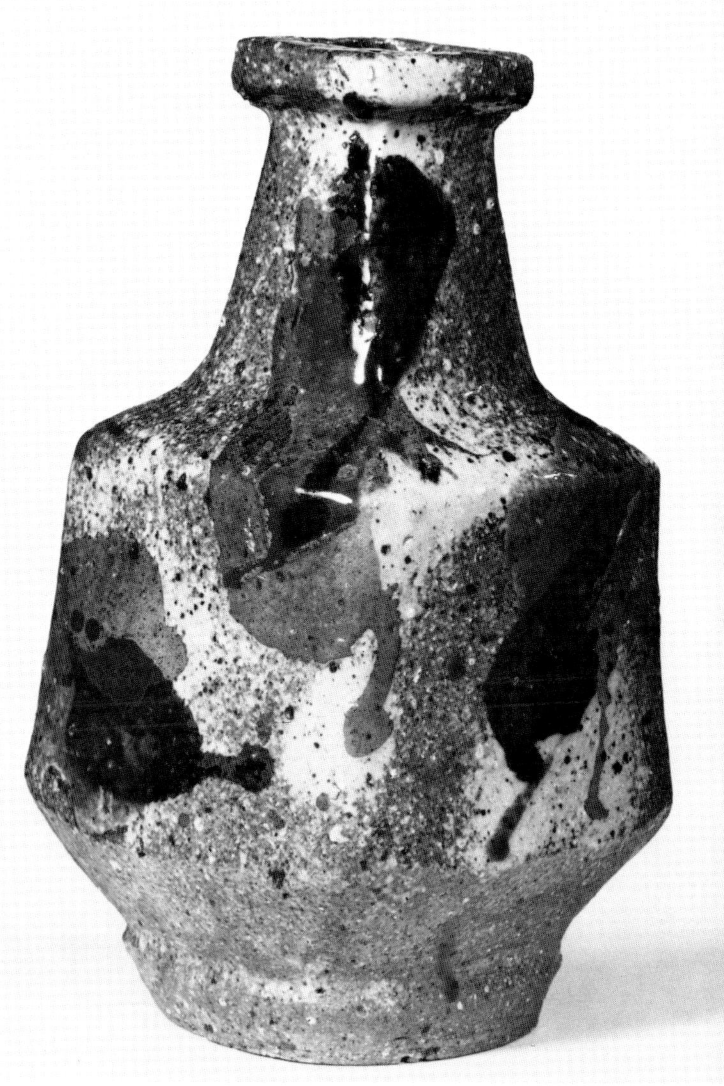

63
Blue-and-White Porcelain Lamp Base
Shōwa Period, *circa* 1945.
Kitaoji Rosanjin 1883–1959.
H: 27.0 cm. (10⅝ in.).
Underglaze cobalt-painted poem and artist's seal; base perforated for lamp cord before glazing.
Published: The Ceramic Art of Kitaoji Rosanjin: Three American Collections (San Francisco, 1964), no. 57; Sidney Cardozo, *Rosanjin: 20th-Century Master Potter of Japan* (New York, 1972), no. 3.
Museum Purchase 75.128.1

64
Kutani-Style Plate
Shōwa Period, *circa* 1950.
Kitaoji Rosanjin 1883–1959.
Diam: 21.6 cm. (8½ in.).
Stoneware dish with brown glaze (except on portion with red and green enamel checkerboard pattern over a clear glaze).
Gift of Dr. Hugo Munsterberg 77. 136

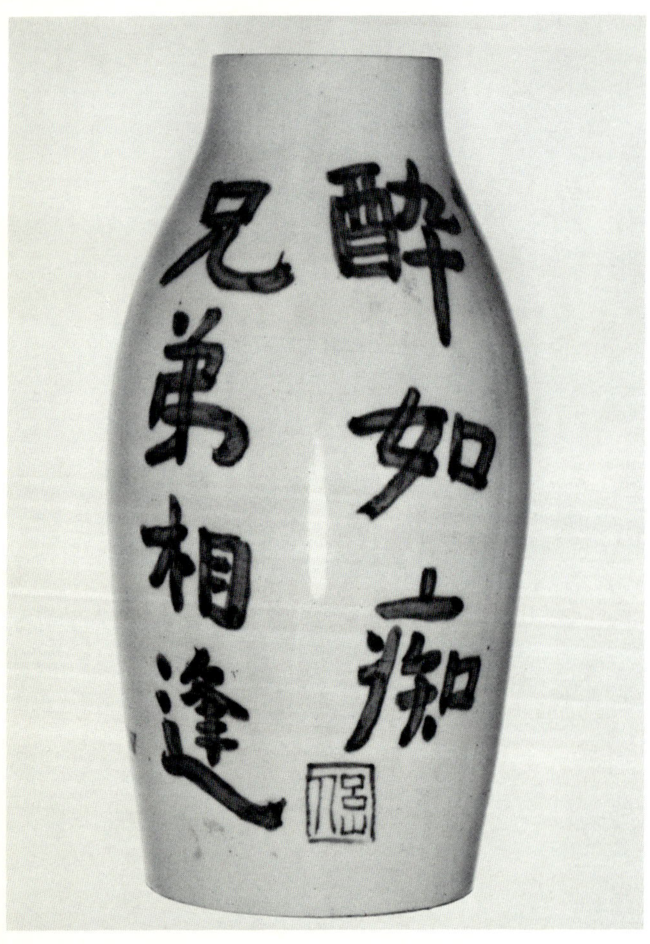

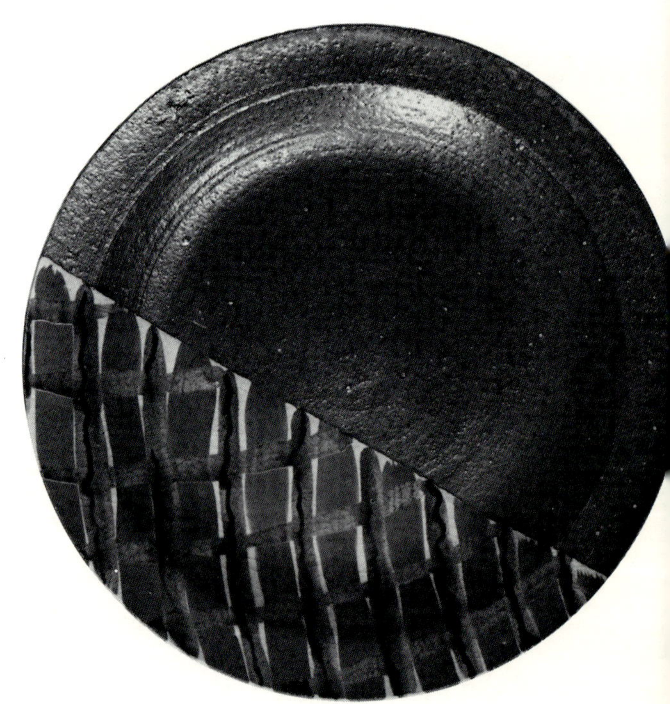

65
Bizen-Style Square Plate
Shōwa Period, *circa* 1950.
Kitaoji Rosanjin 1883–1959.
W: 34.3 cm. (13½ in.).
Gray stoneware platter, exposed surface reddish brown; corners dipped in greenish yellow ash glaze.
Lent by Sidney Cardozo L76.15.25

66
E-Shino *Hi-Ire* (Small Brazier)
Shōwa Period, *circa* 1955.
Kitaoji Rosanjin 1883–1959.
H: 9.5 cm. (3¾ in.).
Buff stoneware with a thick, cream-white Shino glaze; underglaze iron-painted trellis design.
Gift of Dr. Hugo Munsterberg 76.68

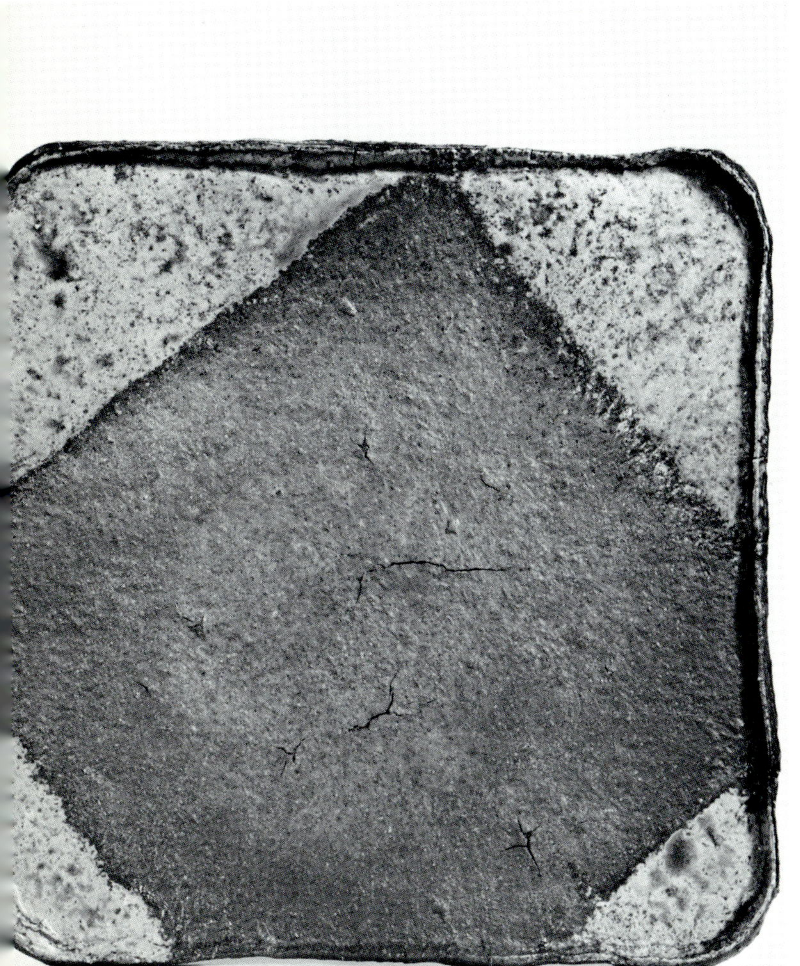

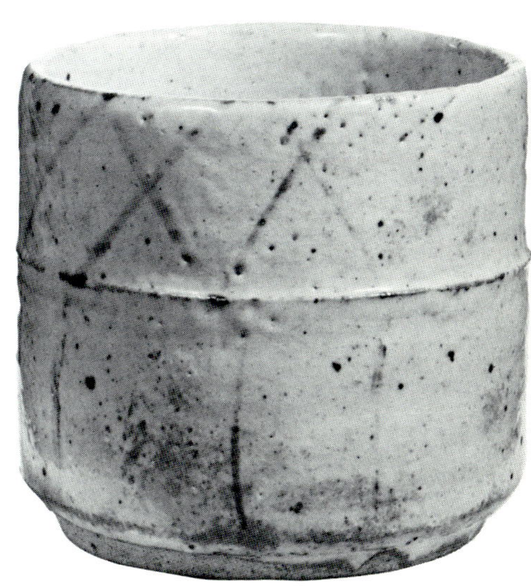

67
Gray Shino Tea Bowl
Shōwa Period, *circa* 1955.
Kitaoji Rosanjin 1883–1959.
H: 7.6 cm. (3 in.).
Iron slip under a thick Shino glaze that appears nearly white where very thick, gray where thinner, and red-brown where thinnest.
Anonymous Gift 72.162.1

68
Oribe Fan-Shaped Dish
Shōwa Period, *circa* 1950.
Kitaoji Rosanjin 1883–1959.
W: 25.4 cm. (10 in.).
Tan stoneware with a cream-colored transparent glaze over an iron-brown painted design of plovers and reeds; upper portion dipped in dark green glaze.
Lent by Sidney Cardozo L76.15.27

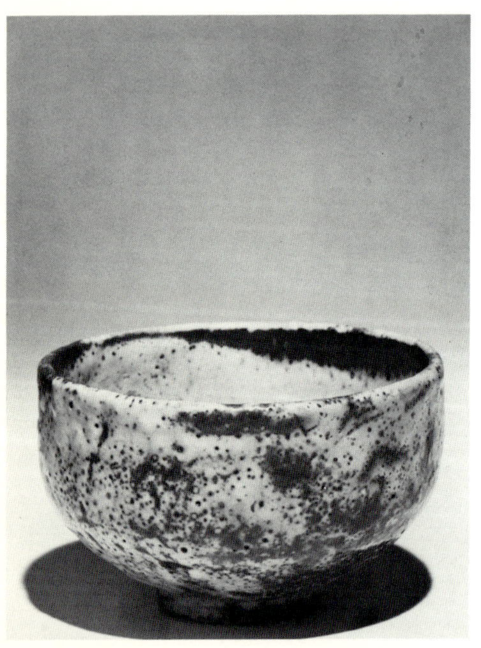

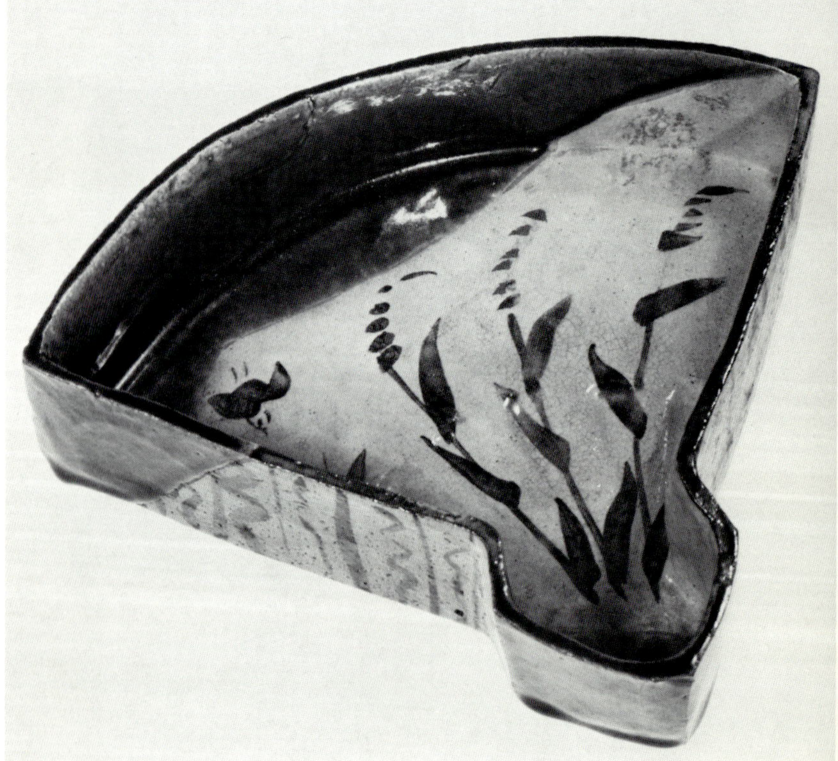

69
Large Stoneware Bowl with Grape Design
Shōwa Period, *circa* 1950.
Kitaoji Rosanjin 1883–1959.
Diam: 23.2 cm. (9⅛ in.).
Buff stoneware with iron-oxide brown-black painting under a clear glaze.
Published: Sidney Cardozo, *Rosanjin: 20th-Century Master Potter of Japan* (New York, 1972), no. 111.
Gift of Sidney Cardozo in memory of Eva M. Cardozo 76.42.1

70
Gray Shino *Kōgō* (Incense Box) **in the Form of a Persimmon**
Shōwa Period, *circa* 1956.
Arakawa Toyozō born 1894.
Diam: 6.0 cm. (2⅜ in.).
Buff stoneware with a milky, semiopaque Shino glaze over iron slip, which shows gray where the glaze is thicker and dark reddish brown where it is thinner or absent.
Gift of Ellen Conant 76.207

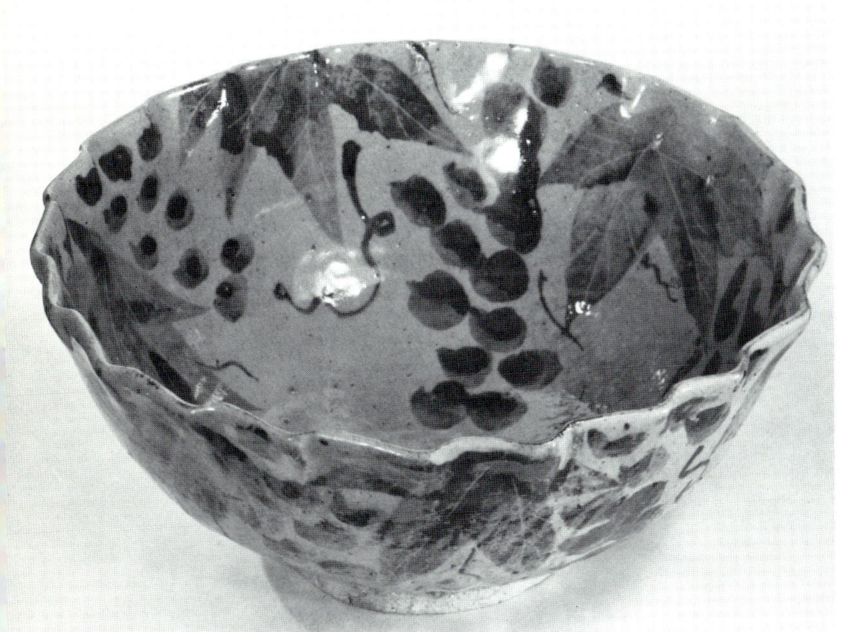

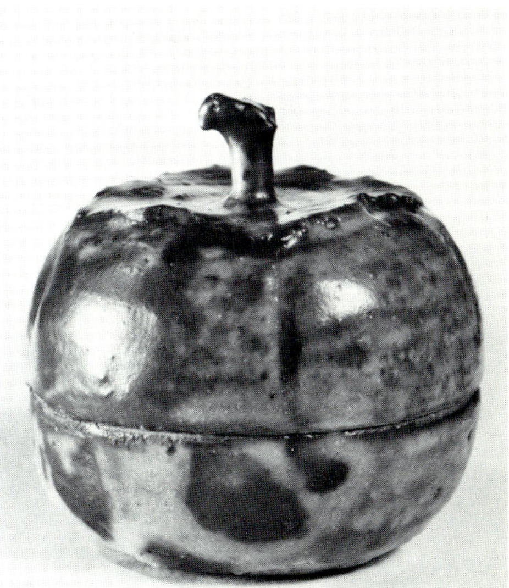

71
Bizen Ware Basin with *Hidasuki* (Salt Water–Dipped Straw) **Markings**
Shōwa Period, *circa* 1960.
Kaneshige Tōyō 1896–1967.
Diam: 36.8 cm. (14½ in.).
Unglazed gray stoneware with reddish buff surface and glossy red straw markings.
Museum Purchase 75.35.2

72
E-Karatsu Dish with Design of Grasses
Shōwa Period, *circa* 1970.
Nakazato Taroemon (Muan) born 1895.
Diam: 24.5 cm. (9⅝ in.).
Gray-buff stoneware with iron-oxide brown-black painting under a clear glaze.
Museum Purchase 75.35.1

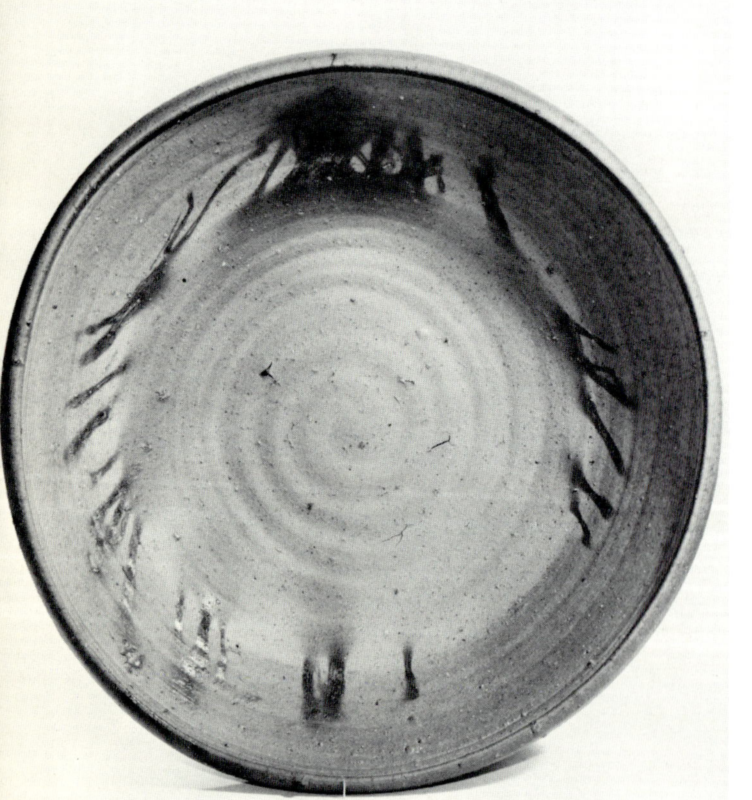

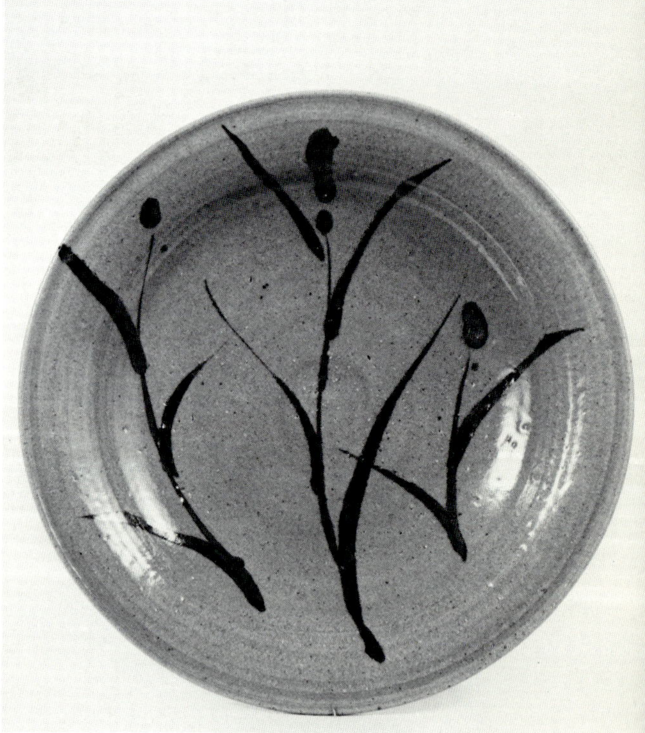

73
Yunomi (Cup for Green Tea)
Shōwa Period, *circa* 1960.
Shimaoka Tatsuzō born 1920.
H: 9.5 cm. (3¾ in.).
Gray stoneware with slip-inlaid pressed-cord pattern and plum blossom crests under a semitransparent glaze.
Lent by Charles Brandon L78.50
[Shimaoka was one of Hamada's best pupils before establishing his own kiln at Mashiko. His father's profession was making braided silk *kimono* cord like that used to impress the design on this cup.]

74
Bizen Ware Jar
Shōwa Period, *circa* 1975.
Konishi Tōzō born 1947.
H: 29.2 cm. (11½ in.).
Stoneware with an eggplant reddish brown surface and a yellowish tan natural ash glaze on the shoulder.
Gift of the Mary Livingston Griggs and Mary Griggs Burke Foundation 76.12
[Konishi Tōzō is one of the best younger Bizen potters. He was born in Imbe, the town that has been the center of Bizen Ware production for centuries.]

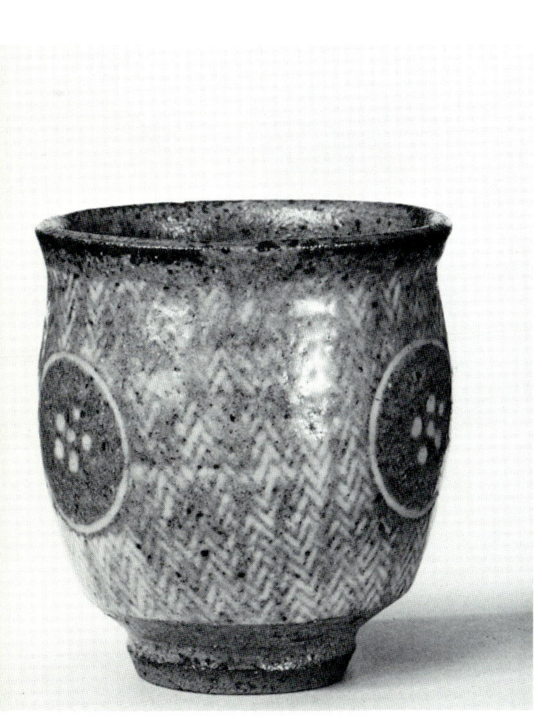

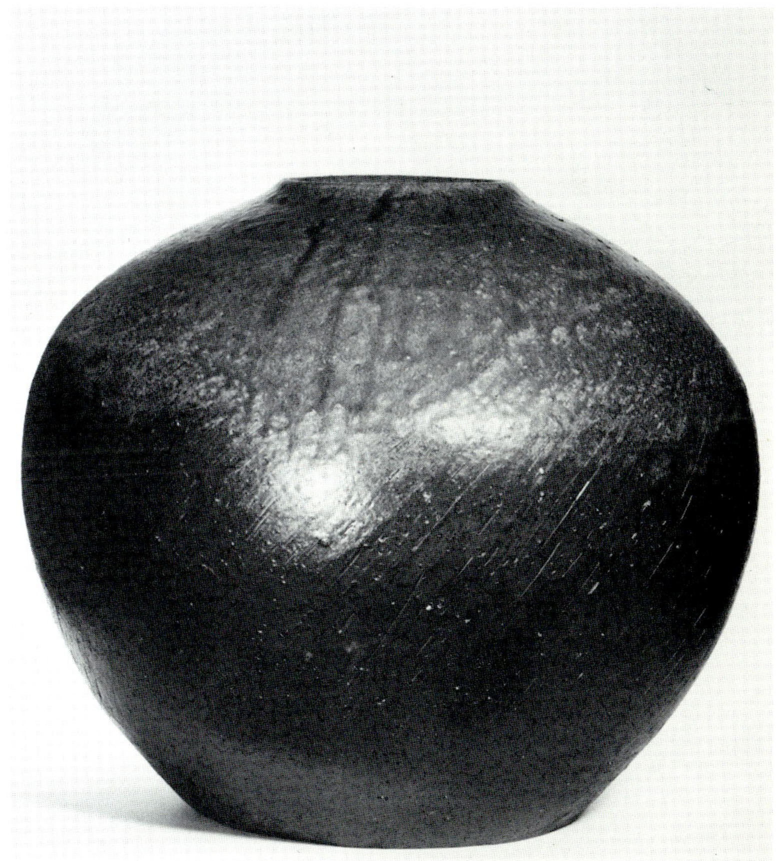

75

Hanging Flower Vase

Shōwa Period, *circa* 1973.

Nakamura Kimpei born 1935.

H: 42.5 cm. (16¾ in.).

Slab-built stoneware with mottled blue glaze.

Anonymous Gift 76.114.1

[Nakamura Kimpei is one of Japan's better-known avant-garde potters. Many of his works are really ceramic sculptures rather than vessels.]

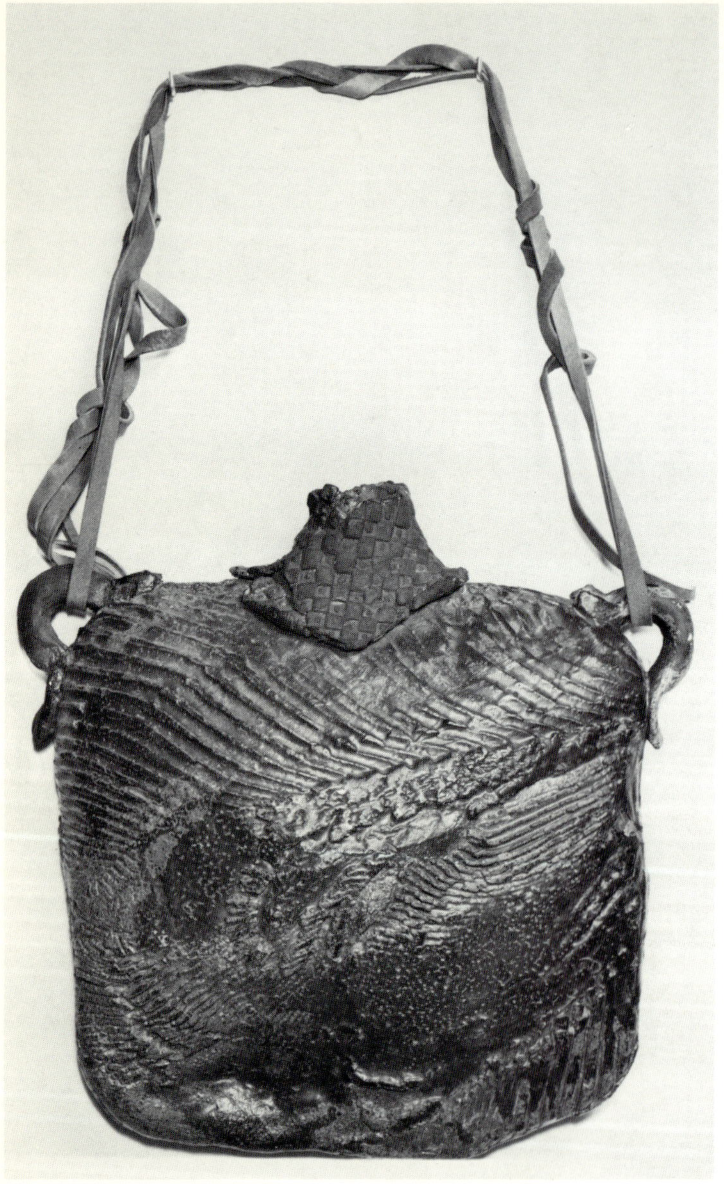

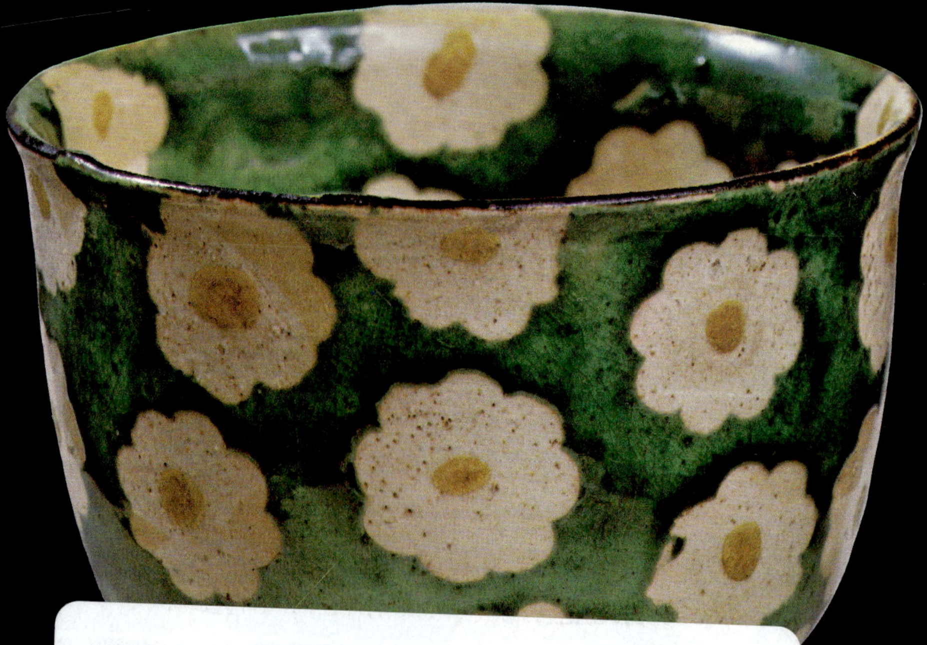